KT-119-163

FOUR SEASONS
of TRAVEL

Come fall, the trees lining
Michigan's Lower Au Sable
River glow brightly.

FOUR SEASONS
of
TRAVEL

400 OF THE WORLD'S BEST DESTINATIONS IN WINTER, SPRING, SUMMER, AND FALL

Foreword by Andrew Evans, *National Geographic Traveler* magazine
contributing editor and "Digital Nomad"

NATIONAL GEOGRAPHIC

WASHINGTON, D.C.

In Provence, the lavender and sunflowers of Plateau de Valensole—derived from the Latin for "valley of the sun"—luxuriate beneath the summer sun.

CONTENTS

True to its name, the Seventh Heaven Express slope near Whistler, Canada, offers spectacular winter skiing.

FOREWORD

By Andrew Evans, *National Geographic Traveler* magazine
contributing editor and "Digital Nomad"

N
OWHERE FEELS COLDER than St. Petersburg in late December. Ice cuts my lungs at every breath, and my chest aches from the severe subzero air. The pastel mansions look like petit fours that line the frozen Moyka, now a slab of solid white ice that frames the original noble city of Peter the Great.

Two minutes on the street is all I can handle. Seeking warmth, I dip into a tea shop where people keep their coats on and sip cups of strong black chai that flows from the bubbling copper samovar. "Come back in June," says the red-faced waitress, "for White Nights." She describes the long summer sun, but for now, I am happy to know these short white days of winter, when Russia turns clean and quiet.

Winter is my favorite season—until spring arrives and Holland explodes into the colored stripes of endless tulip fields. Now is the time to relive my Boy Scout thrills of shooting heavy rapids in West Virginia or return to my youth in France and the vivid spectacle of wailing Romanies as they parade a painted effigy of St. Sara into the milky blue Mediterranean of Saintes-Maries-de-la-Mer.

Summer brings a new celebration of life, with state fairs and street carnivals, warm nights for stargazing, and rambling bears in the woods. And yet just when I am convinced that these warmer months are my favorite, fall arrives with its red glow and ready vineyards.

Travel offers us an eclectic calendar of changing moods, when time and place converge into the perfect moment. Those of us who wander are destined to discover the splendor of each season, whether it's a stampede of zebras kicking up clouds of dust or the glistening blue ice of the Antarctic summer.

This book explores the beauty of the right place at the right time: Kenya's mass gathering of pink flamingos, Polynesia when the air turns sweet with vanilla flowers, Norway's northern lights, India's elaborate monsoon weddings, and Venice dressed in mysterious masquerade. These pages celebrate the span of seasons across the globe and offer up the simple reminder that it's not just where you go—but when.

Travel offers us an eclectic calendar of changing moods, when time and place converge into the perfect moment.

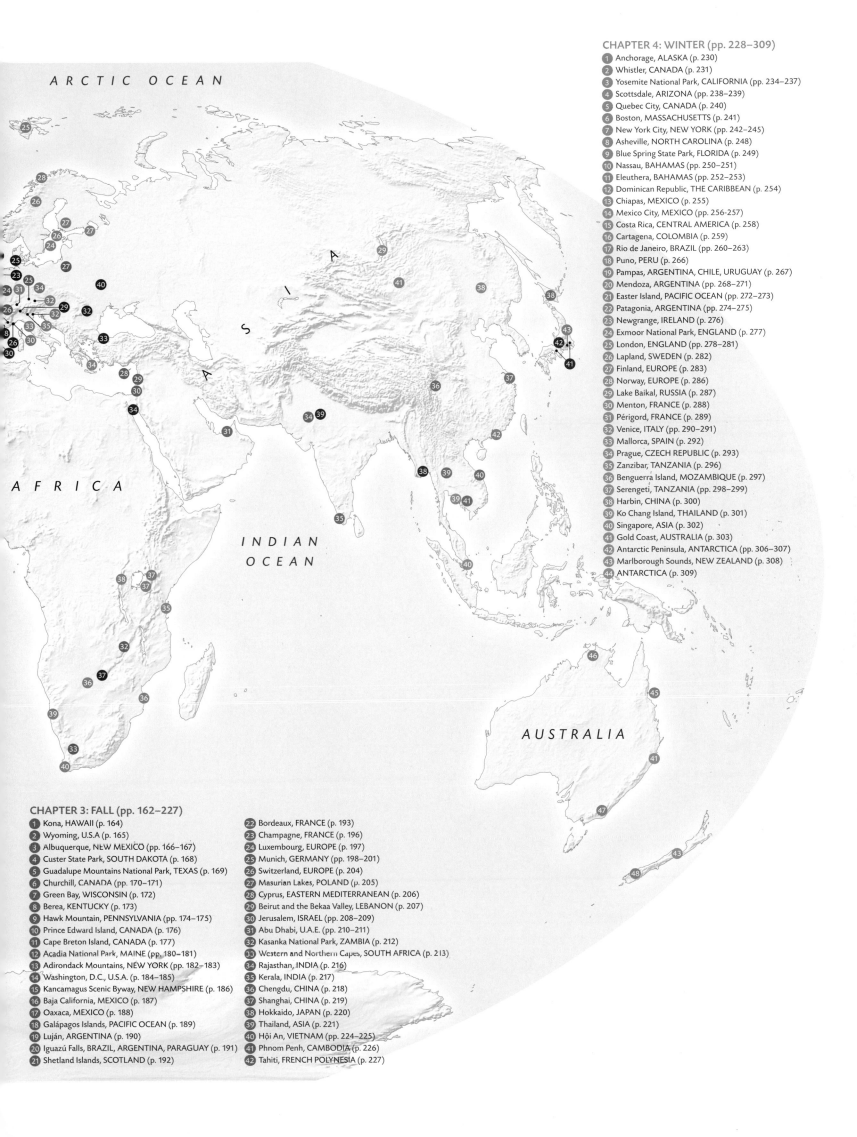

ARCTIC OCEAN

ASIA

AFRICA

INDIAN OCEAN

AUSTRALIA

SPR

BUDDING BLOSSOMS, ANIMALS
ON THE MARCH, CARIBBEAN
REEFS, AND WORLD MUSIC

ING

Nagoya Castle, a 17th-century fortress, now stands watch over the (short-lived) invasion of cherry blossoms each spring.

CALIFORNIA

SAN JUAN CAPISTRANO

Join the swallows that migrate to this ancient mission each spring.

The swallows don't really come to Mission San Juan Capistrano on the same day every year. Legend says the magic day is March 19, St. Joseph's Day, but like any party, some show up early, some show up late, and, let's face it, birds aren't that big on watching the calendar anyway. Which is a good thing: It gives admirers more time to see them as they fill the old mission.

For a century or more, people have described the city's sky around St. Joseph's Day as black with swallows, and the adobe walls of San Juan Capistrano seemed like they'd been built by ancients just as a place for the birds to perch. Today, as you hear the mission bells, you can imagine the sounds of the swallows singing along. In the tiny, narrow Serra Chapel in front of the gold-decked altar, visitors leave candles that flicker like flitting wings.

Fewer and fewer swallows have been showing up over the past years. The mission is doing everything to bring them back so that the springtime music of thousands of them singing into the chapel's open windows never stops.

PLANNING San Juan Capistrano www.sanjuancapistrano.org. **Mission** www.missionsjc.com. About an hour's drive south of Los Angeles, the mission is in the city center.

IN THE KNOW
The Mission Trail

San Juan Capistrano is the seventh of 21 missions making up California's mission trail, which traces the old El Camino Real. Stretching from San Diego to north of San Francisco, the missions were built by the Spanish between the late 1700s and early 1800s, each roughly a day's journey apart and designed to be almost an independent city, with farms, smithies, and workshops. The churches themselves run from quiet chapels to huge, busy buildings with daily services, all lit by tiny windows and spring light. A trip along the trail, mostly following U.S. Highway 101, opens up the heart of the state. www.parks.ca.gov

The San Juan de Capistrano mission bells silently wait for the legendary swallows to come back to roost.

One of the sure signs of spring's arrival in southern Idaho: pronghorn blazing trails through the remaining snow

IDAHO

CRATERS OF THE MOON

Catch the pronghorn migration across the lunar landscape of a western national monument.

You'll always find an otherworldly vista at Idaho's Craters of the Moon National Monument and Preserve. But visit the vast lava field park during a brief window in March and April and the scene becomes alive with pronghorn. The deerlike animals amble along a narrow corridor, making their way from their winter feeding grounds to their summer range in the Pioneer Mountains. (In October, the migration reverses.)

While the several hundred pronghorn don't sprint through the park, they don't dilly-dally either. Luckily they're creatures of habit, and their route paralleling U.S. Highways 20/26/93 doesn't vary. "The path they take is so precise and ingrained, you can see it on Google Earth," says monument wildlife biologist Todd Stefanic. A distinct species closely related to the giraffe, pronghorn indeed look out of Africa, with discrete white striping on their necks.

The challenge for pronghorn-watchers is timing. The creatures move in groups over a period of a month or so. They can be spotted from a car or after a short hike across the windswept sagebrush plain. But don't expect to get closer than 100 yards (90 m)—pronghorn are easily spooked and are among the fastest creatures on Earth, reaching speeds of more than 50 miles an hour (80 kph).

PLANNING Craters of the Moon National Monument and Preserve www.nps.gov/crmo/nature science. The migration period is quite short. For updates, call the park at (208) 527-1335.

IN THE KNOW
Hemingway's Idaho

Ernest Hemingway may have drunk in Havana and caroused in Paris, but he retreated to Idaho. The novelist bought his house in the late 1950s and lived his last years in Ketchum, about 90 minutes from Craters of the Moon. It's easy to see the appeal. Hemingway enjoyed the glamour of nearby Sun Valley Resort, where he spent time with movie stars like Gary Cooper and Ingrid Bergman. But he also cherished the small-town anonymity of Ketchum. He was happiest hunting and fishing in nearby mountains and valleys, including spring-fed Silver Creek, a pinnacle of trout fishing. Hemingway's son Jack helped create a nature preserve there. The author's grave is in Ketchum, encircled by three towering evergreens. www.nature.org

Along with Roosevelt's popular bison and prairie dogs, upward of 100 feral horses roam the park's lands—and, at times, roads.

NORTH DAKOTA

THEODORE ROOSEVELT NATIONAL PARK

Hike through prairie and past stunning geologic formations to a petrified forest.

Though it's in North Dakota, the least visited of all U.S. states (an honor it certainly doesn't deserve), Theodore Roosevelt National Park isn't immune to the crowds that hit the road during the summer travel season. And winters get—and stay—chilly. Late spring is the time to see the park's lesser known badlands and its abundance of wildlife (bison, wild horses, prairie dogs). "The North Dakota badlands is where Theodore Roosevelt turned from 'a skinny scrawny New York dude' into a 'cowboy,' " says Eileen Andes, the park's chief of interpretation and public affairs. It's also, she adds, where Roosevelt's "ideas about conservation began to solidify."

Drive through the South Unit entrance—the preseason quiet allows time for a nice chat with the ranger—and take a quick left into the Medora visitor center. There, gather intel (a trail map, directions to the Peaceful Valley Ranch trailhead) and fill your water bottles. A short drive and moderately challenging hike to one of the country's largest concentrations of petrified wood is ahead. It's doubtful you'll see anybody else as you walk through tall prairie grass and pass by otherworldly geologic formations—"It's in the wilderness area," Andes notes—then, on to the Petrified Forest, with its massive pieces of no-longer-wood, including plenty of standing stumps. Adds Andes: "It's a really special collection."

PLANNING Theodore Roosevelt National Park www.nps.gov/thro. Consider staying at the Rough Riders Hotel *(www.medora.com/rough-riders),* named for Roosevelt's Spanish-American War regiment.

GREAT STAYS
Cottonwood Campground

The evenings get cool, but it's nothing a fleece jacket, some fingerless gloves, and a good campfire can't cure. And even mild discomfort will be wiped away from your mind at the first sighting of the park's bison herd wandering through the campground. It's easy to understand why so many people return to this park campground year after year. The slower spring season will make it easier to land one of the first-come first-served spots at the back of the loops, where your view will feature badlands and the Little Missouri River. Not bad for ten bucks a night. www.nps.gov/thro/planyourvisit/camping.htm

TENNESSEE

NASHVILLE

Listen up as big music stars and their hit songwriters play their tunes on stages all over town.

Between attention for its eponymous hit TV show and its better-than-ever food scene, few U.S. cities have been hotter than Nashville during the last few years. Some of its best rewards come from a springtime visit, when the temps are walk-around perfect and, thanks to the Tin Pan South Songwriters Festival, the city's best crop—songwriters—is in full bloom.

Stretching over five nights, Tin Pan South hits music venues around town. Stages are loaded with everybody from big-name singer-songwriters to songwriters whose work turned singers into big names (from country to rock and beyond). And after hearing them play their tunes, you'll remember their names.

Though songwriting is a competitive industry, it's also one of Nashville's strongest communities. "Any [Tin Pan South] audience is 50 percent people who want to be songwriters, 40 percent fans, and 10 percent other songwriters going in and supporting their friends," says Grammy-winning songwriter Tia Sillers.

Tin Pan South energizes even industry vets. "I went to Nashville many years after I had my greatest success," says Paul Williams, Academy Award–winning songwriter and president of the American Society of Composers, Authors, and Publishers. "But I feel my real love affair with music—the birthplace of that—is Tin Pan South."

PLANNING Nashville www.visitmusiccity.com. **Tin Pan South Songwriters Festival** www.tinpansouth.com.

FOR FOODIES
Nashville Farmers' Market

From the collards at Jamaicaway to the day's specials at Nashville star chef Arnold Myint's AM@FM, there are fields' upon fields' worth of springtime, locally sourced strawberries, turnip greens, and more on the menus of the food stalls and restaurants of Nashville Farmers' Market. After grazing your way around, cross into the farm-stand building where the growers offer up more goodies so you can cook your own Southern spring masterpieces. Or, at least, photograph them. Drove into town? Make sure you leave plenty of room in the trunk for your market haul: Fresh greens take up some serious space. nashville farmersmarket.org

Musicians muscle their instruments across Nashville's Broadway, likely bound for one of the world-famous honky-tonks that line "Lower Broad."

INDIANAPOLIS, INDIANA

INDIANAPOLIS 500

"When the drivers round Turn 4, the green flag snaps and what sounds like the drone of a muscular swarm of 1,600-pound [726 kg] metal hornets screams past the stands, releasing a most hellacious noise. It is very loud and very scary—and extremely exciting."

—GARY MCKECHNIE, AUTHOR OF NATIONAL GEOGRAPHIC'S *USA 101*

First held in 1911, the Indianapolis 500 takes place on the last weekend in May at the Indianapolis Motor Speedway (the largest sporting spectator facility in the world). *Pictured:* Sam Hornish, Jr., tears around a turn.

MEMPHIS

Devour some of the blues capital's best local 'cue during the barbecue world championships in May.

IN THE KNOW
Beale Street Blues

The South doesn't feel quite right when the heat isn't on. But *too* hot, and the day is cooked. So, May, with highs in the low 80s°F (high 20s°C) and, better, a barbecue festival, promises some serious sweet heat.

When it comes to Memphis's dedication to barbecue, there's no contest. "Two things Memphis is known for: churches and barbecue restaurants on every corner," says Ron Childers, a certified barbecue contest judge and meteorologist for WMC-TV. So it's fitting that the city hosts the World Championship Barbecue Cooking Contest every May. One of the premier events on the BBQ cooking contest circuit, the championship welcomes smokers of all shapes and sizes—BBQ smokers, that is—ready to put their recipes to the test and, tongs crossed, bag some bragging rights. Contestants can't feed the public (health laws won't have it). But competitors do right by your eyes by dressing up their tents and smokers; Childers remembers a group of pilots who built a smoker shaped like a miniature airplane.

To actually feast on some 'cue, head to one of Memphis's many great barbecue restaurants. You can get excellent chicken or beef, but Childers recommends the classic cuts. "Memphis-style barbecue is pork ribs, pork shoulder, or whole hog. Pork and a sweet rub."

Sounds like a winner.

PLANNING Memphis www.memphistravel.com. **World Championship Barbecue Cooking Contest** www.memphisinmay.org.

Beale Street was calling them. During the first half of the 1900s, the Memphis street that stretches nearly 2 miles (3 km) from the Mississippi River became the go-to locale for musicians who wanted to make names for themselves. Early on, an upbeat blues style emerged. After World War II, things took a harder edge and musicians, including Howlin' Wolf and B. B. King, went from being Beale Street players to internationally famed household names. The street's appeal still holds true—though it has more of a touristy vibe than it did in decades past. Go anyway. Venues offer everything from Memphis blues to its offspring, rock and roll. www.bealestreetonline.com, www.bealestreet.com

Look for hot barbecue turkey drumsticks or baby back ribs on Memphis menus.

The New Orleans Jazz and Heritage Festival in 2012 featured guitarist Vasti Jackson among its many talented performers.

LOUISIANA

NEW ORLEANS

Overwhelm your senses at the Jazz Fest, where legendary sounds mix with the city's rich cultural gumbo.

Jazz is one of many musical styles that bursts the sound barrier of the New Orleans Fair Grounds Race Course, where thousands gather for the annual Jazz Fest. Its official title—the New Orleans Jazz and Heritage Festival—is more apt. Indigenous genres like Cajun and zydeco are performed alongside contemporary international styles equally alive in the city—all at a festival that pays tribute to the larger culinary, linguistic, artistic, and cultural traditions with which music is always entwined. The late April festival—perched on the brink of summer, just before the swampy Louisiana heat sets it—has been held since 1970, drawing A-listers like Bruce Springsteen and Jimmy Buffett, as well as big-name New Orleans legends like Fats Domino and the Preservation Hall Jazz Band.

The best way to experience it is to meander, exposing your ear to the festival's 12 stages and countless impromptu musical shows that erupt next to, behind, and in between them. "You'll experience a little bit of everything: gospel, rock, blues, zydeco, funk, African, Latin, brass, R&B," says annual festivalgoer Monica Corcoran, plus "the traveling brass bands, second-liners, and Mardi Gras Indians that weave their way among the crowds, carrying people along with their music."

PLANNING New Orleans Jazz and Heritage Festival www.nojazzfest.com. Tickets may be purchased at most Ticketmaster outlets, online, or at the New Orleans Arena.

IN THE KNOW
The George Wein Legacy

The New Orleans Jazz and Heritage Festival was the brainchild of George Wein, founder of the legendary Newport Jazz Festival in Rhode Island. When Wein presented his first Newport festival in 1954, it was a groundbreaking platform for jazz musicians to reach wider audiences at a time when they were largely relegated to dusty nightclubs. By the time he was hired to produce the New Orleans Jazz Fest in 1970, the genre had gained widespread popularity. Recognizing the reach of jazz in New Orleans, Wein conceived of an event to celebrate the music within the larger context of the city's vibrant culture that nourished—and continues to nourish—it today.

Lisa Ling

Austin's South by Southwest

As soon as my husband Paul and I boarded our flight from Los Angeles to Austin, Texas, and looked around at all the artist types traveling to the Longhorn City, we knew we were going to be doing something cool. Every year in the early spring, Brooklynites, Angelinos, and young hipsters from all over the country and world flee their hometowns and head to Austin for the South by Southwest music, film, and interactive technology festival. Regulars refer to the trifecta of events as "Southby."

Southby takes place over the course of a week and a half, usually starting in early March. The festival is undeniably a colossal party scene. But the days are filled with speakers, workshops, and an exhibit hall for those who want to learn more about any or all of the three different genres. Music starts midway through and ends the festival.

I was blown away by the throngs of young, aspiring Internet and gaming entrepreneurs who show up with hopes of debuting their ideas and becoming the next Mark Zuckerberg—who has been a speaker at Southby. After all, it was here in 2007 that one of the biggest social networks on Earth, Twitter, was introduced to the world. It was so interesting to see thousands of college kids, college dropouts, and ambitious young people working the rooms trying to make it big in an industry that barely existed 20 years ago.

After the tech festival came to a close, we readied ourselves for some long nights of shots and amazing music. With huge mainstream acts like Jay-Z, the Foo Fighters, Metallica, and the White Stripes, as well as legendary and indie rockers, Austin's stages and bars come alive. Every bar in Central Austin hosts a series of bands, and we came across sounds that we'd never heard before. Though I'd seen probably 15 bands over the course of several days, as someone who came of age in the '80s, the highlight for me was seeing my first crushes, Duran Duran. It was hot, sweaty, and way overcrowded, but the wild boys—or slightly old men by now—didn't disappoint.

Big note for those wanting to experience Southby: Wear comfortable shoes!

Lisa Ling is the executive producer and host of Our America *on the Oprah Winfrey Network. She also hosts CBS TV's* The Job.

"*I was blown away by the throngs of young, aspiring … entrepreneurs who show up with hopes of … becoming the next Mark Zuckerberg.*"

From start-up companies to bands on the cusp, Austin's "Southby" showcases the next big new. Here, the Pipettes blow it up in their trademark polka dots.

In an age-old tradition, farmers near West Brattleboro, Vermont, collect sap with the help of a horse-drawn gathering tank.

UNITED STATES

VERMONT

Indulge in the sticky, naturally sweet tastes and aromas of fresh maple syrup during its spring coming out party.

At the time when most farmers are just beginning to think about spring planting, maple syrup producers across Vermont are already enjoying their harvests. Vermont leads the country in syrup production with an ideal combination of climate, soil, and aged trees. Syrup season climaxes with the Vermont Maple Festival, a nearly half-century-old tradition in the northern town of St. Albans, where visitors gather to taste all four grades of Vermont's legendary syrup, each with a distinct bouquet, body, taste, and finish. "Everyone tries the syrups in little cups, starting with the lighter grades and moving to the darker," says festival cochair Carolyn Perley. Like the other planners of the volunteer-run festival, the Perleys are sugarmakers.

To best see syrupmaking in action, arrive before the April festival. Syrup season begins when spring's first breath warms the thaw just enough to awaken the dormant trees and start sap pumping. Snow still conceals the forest floors when sugarmakers trek into the woods to tap the trees. Sap is collected and boiled in sugarhouses, creating clouds of steam laced with sweet aromas. In order to bear the label "Vermont Maple Syrup," all syrup must be 100 percent natural with nothing added.

PLANNING **Vermont Maple Festival** www.vtmaplefestival.org. **Vermont's maple syrup season** www.vermontmaple.org. Many of Vermont's sugarhouses are open to the public, some seasonally and others throughout the year.

GREAT STAYS
Eat, Sleep, Learn, and Play on a Vermont Farm

● **FOUR SPRINGS FARM:** A single-owner farm with a cabin and campground. Immerse yourself in farm life by helping out with the morning chores or picking your own vegetables. www.fourspringsfarm.com

● **HOLLISTER HILL FARM:** A small, family-run farm with four dairy cows that supply raw milk to farm customers. Stay in an early 19th-century farmhouse and spend your mornings in the barn feeding and watering the animals. www.hollisterhillfarm.com

● **TREVIN FARMS:** A working farm with chickens, horses, goats, and chemical-free vegetable gardens. Spend the morning gathering eggs from the henhouse for breakfast and milking the goats to gather the milk you'll use later at cheesemaking class. www.trevinfarms.com

UNITED STATES

WEST VIRGINIA

Raft the currents of West Virginia's rivers, renowned for both their beauty and brute force.

IN THE KNOW
Minimizing Risks

Water is a powerful force in the mountains of southern West Virginia, a region threaded with rivers that have been harnessed for industry and recreation alike. At times the rivers twist lackadaisically around soft curves and bends. But know that flows can shift with bipolar rapidity, transforming into roiling hydraulic pools and violent rapids that churn over steep drops.

Spring is the best time to challenge the New River, one of the most popular runs for white-water rafting, as melting snow increases the level and force of the flow. Likewise, the Gauley River holds its own springtime powers, notorious for muscular rapids and steep gradients that draw large crowds in the fall when the dam is opened. "Spring is an open book for us," says river manager Rick Miller. "Fall is predictable, but some of our best trips are in the spring."

Despite their reputations, certain sections of the rivers are better known for their calmer personalities. The upper New River, which cascades through picturesque canyons, is best for beginners. "That's the beauty of the river," says Turner Sharp of the West Virginia Rivers Coalition. "It's flowing all the time. But when you go slower, you get to enjoy the scenery."

Though enjoyed by thousands of enthusiasts and beginners alike each season, white-water rafting is risky. If you've never rafted before, start easy and get a taste of the experience. As you must always be prepared to swim a rapid if the raft capsizes, assess your health and physical limitations before making a decision about which run to take. Beyond personal safety, increased tourism from the rafting industry carries environmental risks as well. Carpool to rafting sites in order to reduce your carbon footprint, and consider camping away from the river to reduce degradation of the riverbanks.

PLANNING West Virginia white-water rafting wvcommerce.org. Wildwater Expeditions *(www.wvaraft .com)* is the oldest rafting outfitter in West Virginia and the force that jump-started the industry.

Adventurists paddle their way through the mist kicked up by West Virginia's powerful Gauley River.

VIRGINIA

Taste your way through the Old Dominion's pastoral wine country, rooted in American history and celebrated with spring festivals.

Resting in the foothills of the Blue Ridge, the mansion of James Madison, the United States' fourth President, provides a majestic backdrop for one of the oldest celebrations of Virginia wine. One of many festivals held each spring to kick off Virginia's wine season, the Montpelier Wine Festival draws local winemakers who present their variations on the theme of Virginia grapes. On the periphery of the 2,700-acre (1,100 ha) estate, families spread picnic blankets accompanied by their bottles of choice.

Virginia's foray into the art of grape cultivation began with U.S. Founding Fathers like Madison, many of whom were well-read agriculturists. With visions of a New World wine industry, Thomas Jefferson planted vineyards at his Monticello estate. Though his grapes failed, Jefferson established a tradition that contemporary winemakers continue to reference.

Events at historic estates convey a sense of past while allowing visitors to sample the varied fruits of local labor and passion. "Dry, fruity, spicy—there's a whole gamut of wines to taste," observes Montpelier's Barbara Bannar. Bannar suggests talking to the outgoing winemakers themselves, who, like their enterprising forefathers, are craftspeople.

PLANNING Virginia wine festivals Montpelier, www.montpelierwinefestival.com; Monticello, monticello winetrailfestival.com; Ash Lawn–Highland, www.ashlawnhighland.org.

IN THE KNOW
The Founding Father of Wine

A lesser known achievement on Thomas Jefferson's impressive résumé is his status as a Founding Father of American wine. The third U.S. President put his heart into his vineyards, but the effort never yielded wine. Jefferson's vines were revived in the mid-1980s by Italian-born viticulturist Gabriele Rausse, who grafted and replanted the original varieties at Monticello. "Jefferson planted tobacco first," Rausse recounts, but soon realized that tobacco ruined the soil and advocated grapes as an alternative. "But nobody listened, and the future of Virginia was tobacco." Two centuries and 200 wineries later, Virginia is now listening to Jefferson.

Quench your thirst with vino that owes its existence to a winemaking tradition inspired by Thomas Jefferson's agricultural aspirations.

The crowd goes quiet waiting to see if the seventh green at Augusta National Golf Club will be kind to the next competitor.

GEORGIA

AUGUSTA

Watch golf's superstars play the famed greens of Augusta in a gracious, historic Southern city.

Every April, just as the azaleas begin to bud, the storied Masters Tournament brings the world's top golfers to east Georgia. While the private Augusta National Golf Club closely guards the coveted badges for admittance to the four-day contest, the unwashed have a chance to step onto the fabled grounds during three days of practice rounds. Tickets are distributed by lottery, and the lucky winners get a chance to watch the sport's top players chip, drive, and putt around golf's most famous—and some say most beautiful—course. Highlights include Magnolia Lane, the club entryway, lined by trees that create a stunning springtime allée; Rae's Creek, the course's lowest point, into which many a rueful player has watched his ball roll; and Butler Cabin, from where TV broadcasts the tournament each year.

Take advantage of one beautiful spring day to explore the city itself, when Augusta is "almost Caribbean," claims Brad Usry, a lifetime resident and owner of the popular soul food joint Fat Man's Mill Café. "Dogwoods in bloom, mild mornings, flowers shining in warm sunlight. The climate is blissful, and folks are happy." Take a quiet stroll along the Savannah River on the Riverwalk, visit the city's magnificent antebellum mansions, and check out the boyhood home of President Woodrow Wilson.

PLANNING Augusta www.augustaga.gov. **Masters Tournament** masters.com. Online lottery registration for practice-day entry begins shortly after the previous year's tournament ends, but winners are few; try eBay and Craigslist. Note that state law prohibits ticket sales near the course.

GREAT STAYS
The Partridge Inn

More than a century ago, when Georgia reigned as the East Coast's winter vacation capital, the social season revolved around Augusta's Partridge Inn. Constructed as a home in 1836 and later expanded into a 145-room hotel, it has hosted the world's top golfers, celebrities, and U.S. Presidents—as the black-and-white photos on the walls attest.

It still looks the part, with verandas, balconies, and wraparound porches stretching literally a quarter mile (400 m) and sitting in the heart of the hilltop Historic Summerville District. Try the Sunday brunch, a full Deep South spread, from shrimp and grits to, of course, pecan pie for dessert. www.partridgeinn.com

GREAT SMOKY MOUNTAINS NATIONAL PARK

"In the North the spring holds back, then comes with a rush, tumbles its treasures in a heap at your feet, and is gone. Here, the spirit of the South prevails, and the spring gradually unfolds for three months, rising in a strong, slow tide that finally breaks over the land in a tremendous flood of color and fragrance and song."

—MARGARET W. MORLEY, *THE CAROLINA MOUNTAINS* (1913)

Great Smoky Mountains National Park spans more than 800 square miles (2,100 sq km) along the Tennessee–North Carolina border. Initially created in 1934 to protect the land from excessive logging, the park remains home to a biologically diverse 17,000 species of flora and fauna. *Pictured:* Sunrise over the park's Oconaluftee Valley

Even Hawaii's flowers would be jealous of the underwater color blast served up by the Caribbean's fish, coral, and bright orange sea stars.

THE CARIBBEAN

PUERTO RICO

Try snuba to explore the underwater tropical splendor of the Caribbean's great coral reefs.

Just off Puerto Rico's sultry, palm-shaded southern coast, 15 feet (4.5 m) beneath the water's surface, flirt with royal blue sergeant majors, tunnel through staghorn and elkhorn coral, and float across waving sea grass dotted with enormous conch shells. The experience may feel like scuba diving—but it's not. It's snuba.

Developed in 1989, snuba is popular in tropical paradises worldwide. But Puerto Rico—where the U.S. dollar is currency, passports are unnecessary, and English is widely spoken—is a top choice in spring.

The trip begins on a short boat ride from Copamarina Beach Resort in Guánica, during which the bronzed guide tells you the basics. A cross between snorkeling and scuba diving, snuba involves placing in your mouth a breathing device that's attached to an air tank above on a pontoon raft. You have swim fins and a diving mask, but no heavy tanks to carry on your back, and no certificate or prior experience is required. A weight around your waist makes sure you sink to the seafloor.

As you glide through the pellucid waters, the swim becomes a meditation on amazing beauty, on the wonder of sweet rainbow fish darting to and fro, and on the vast blue world all around you.

PLANNING Aqua Adventure at Copamarina Beach Resort www.copamarina.com, www.aquaadventurepr.com.

IN THE KNOW
Hidden Puerto Rico

Puerto Rico's southwest corner remains happily undiscovered. Hike through the cactus-sprinkled Guánica Dry Forest Reserve (with only 30 inches / 76 cm of rain a year, the opposite of a rain forest); paddle to seashell-speckled Gilligan's Island, part of the Biosphere Reserve of Guánica; watch the sun set atop cliffs at the Cabo Rojo lighthouse; or explore the sun-drenched village of Guánica, invaded by American forces in 1898 in the first step of Puerto Rico becoming a U.S. territory. In February, the weeklong Carnaval de Ponce descends on Ponce's colonial core with costumed parades and *bomba y plena* music.

ST. LUCIA

Hike among this tropical island's wild orchids and lush rain forests as spring clears the way.

A tropical paradise of overpowering beauty, the mountainous island of St. Lucia is blessed with some of the Caribbean's most dramatic scenery. Its majestic peaks of Petit and Gros Piton jut from the coast like sugarloaves, while in the interior lie miles and miles of verdant rain forest. The best time to come is April and May, before the summer rainy season begins and between waves of visitors. On hikes, you may have the place to yourself.

The rain forest is a veritable Garden of Eden, laced with 29 miles (47 km) of hiking trails, each one more breathtaking than the last. Fragrant wild orchids, jasmine, and frangipani carpet St. Lucia's fertile soil. Hummingbirds flit among exotic flowering lobster claws beneath a swaying canopy of palms and colorful *dédéfouden* trees. A fitting introduction is the Parrot Trail, a four-hour jaunt near the town of Micoud. "Since Hurricane Tomás hit the opposite coast in 2010, more gorgeous birds have settled here than ever before," says tour guide Fabian Philip. Many come to spot the elusive Amazona versicolor, St. Lucia's indigenous parrot, with its bright blue face, red throat, green wings, and tail dipped in yellow. You can usually hear it shrieking long before it streaks into view.

PLANNING St. Lucia www.visitstlucia.net, www.saintlucia-tourism.com. **Hiking** Fabian Tours, www.fabian toursstlucia.com; ATV Paradise Tours, www.atvstlucia.com.

BEST OF THE BEST
Night Zip-lining

Can't buy a thrill, you say? Try zipping through the rain forest canopy of St. Lucia at full moon. From the northern town of Chassin, guides lead three-hour night excursions to the root-encrusted Eagle's Claw, a volcanic boulder deep in this eco-adventure park. Here, you clamber up a set of "floating steps" to your launch point, hitch up to the cables, and race from tree to tree. Nocturnal creatures blink curiously into the beam of your headlamp. At the last of the platforms—invitingly named the Tarantula's Nest—you rappel back to the jungle floor. www.rainforestadventure.com

St. Lucia's most visible geographic formations, the Pitons are part of a volcanic complex. Their neighbors include fumaroles and hot springs.

THE CARIBBEAN

ANTIGUA

Jump aboard or celebrate dockside during Sailing Week as hundreds of yachts compete in the season's grand, final regatta.

You've sailed before, but nothing like this—a full-scale regatta around the island of Antigua in the eastern Caribbean. Three days of hard-core sailing punctuated by rowdy beach parties at Dickenson Bay and the aptly named Jolly Harbour. And now you're on the home stretch, speeding along the island's southern shore as you make for English Harbour and the finishing line.

Fun in the sun and dead-serious sailing make Antigua's annual Sailing Week at the end of April one of the globe's premier water-sport events. By day, skilled crews compete in 29 categories broken down by size, shape, and national origin of vessel. By night, everyone parties like the dickens on the island's beaches and dockside. Spring weather—after the rainy season and before the hurricanes blow in—provides ideal sailing conditions.

"Antigua Week is one of the most original Caribbean regattas," says Englishman Christian Reynolds, who's raced his 51-foot (16 m) *Northern Child* half a dozen times in the event. Even rookies can get into the action by signing up to crew aboard a yacht in one of the not-so-competitive categories. Nor do landlubbers need to miss out; they can get swept up in the maritime hoopla by attending the parties, concerts, and other special events at Nelson's Dockyard on the island's south coast.

PLANNING Antigua www.antigua-barbuda.org. **Antigua Sailing Week** www.sailingweek.com. A number of boats offer crew positions, including the *Northern Child (www.northernchild.com).*

IN THE KNOW
Lord Nelson in Antigua

Horatio Nelson arrived in Antigua in 1784 as a 26-year-old Royal Navy officer commanding the frigate H.M.S. *Boreas.* He had the unpopular assignment of enforcing the British Navigation Acts and preventing trading with the recently independent United States. For one of the few times in his life, Nelson failed and was even sequestered aboard *Boreas* for eight months facing possible legal action. On the other hand, his social life blossomed. On nearby Nevis, the dashing Nelson met young widow Fanny Nisbet and the two soon married. In the summer of 1787, Nelson sailed back to England, destined for immortality 18 years later at Trafalgar.

In their quest to win the race or, at the very least, keep their boat's speed from flagging, the crew sets to trimming the jib.

With just hours to create a temporary street fresco on Calle de las Alfombras, artists turn sawdust into an eye-catching work of art.

NICARAGUA
LEÓN

Celebrate Holy Week in a town where authentic Latin American ritual fuses with artistic passion.

The hot, steamy intellectual capital of Nicaragua's northwest is something of an unpolished gem, its Spanish colonial churches rubbing shoulders with gritty student bars and peeling revolutionary Sandinista murals. León's earthy traditions are on display during Semana Santa, the authentic Easter rituals marked by slow-moving religious processions, dirges, and wailing among the devout.

On Good Friday, the main avenue erupts into vivid splashes of color called *alfombras de aserrin,* or "sawdust carpets." Working late into the night, and often poring over ragged photos for reference, residents create amazing versions of Jesus, the Virgin Mary, and other sacred motifs from pine needles, flower petals, sand, and dyed sawdust. The method originated in León more than a century ago and, unlike in other places celebrating Holy Week, the artists still work freehand rather than with molds.

"Anyone can claim a space on the street and do it," says Richard Leonardi, general manager at Tours Nicaragua. "Most of these people don't produce art the rest of the year, so it's very democratic." Family members, friends, and onlookers alike offer advice, perhaps on how to improve a halo or crown of thorns. The pieces have an ephemeral quality: Worshippers en route to Good Friday services at León's humongous cathedral trample the creations.

PLANNING León www.visit-nicaragua.com, www.nicaragua.com. **Cultural tours** www.toursnicaragua.com, www.vapues.com. Book hotels well in advance—and watch your valuables; thieves abound during Holy Week.

FOR FOODIES
Central Market

For mouthwatering cuisine during Holy Week, look no farther than León's atmospheric Mercado Central, the central market. Vendors on and around the square will be selling traditional Easter sweets like *huevos chimbos* ("fake eggs" of cane sugar and almonds) and *almibar* (soft mango-chestnut drops) alongside more rustic offerings of *gaspar* (dried salted gar) and *pinol de iguana* (iguana soup). Year-round, sidewalk barbecues serve heaping portions of *gallo pinto* (rice and beans), *papas rellenas* (stuffed potatoes), and *comida corriente,* a fresh spread of whatever's on that day. Wash it all down with popular *chicha,* an unfermented corn drink.

OUTDOOR FLOWER MARKETS

Flood the senses with irresistible blooms by the bucket load, exotic and everyday.

CUENCA FLOWER MARKET

Cuenca, Ecuador

One of the world's great historic cities, Cuenca boasts more than 50 churches from the Spanish colonial era. But its major draw is the daily flower market, lurking in the shadow of the monumental Catedral de la Inmaculada Concepción. Vendors at dozens of stands offer quivering orchids, arum lilies, and giant roses.

www.incuenca.com

MARCHÉ AUX FLEURS

Île de la Cité, Paris, France

Risk sensory overload at the 200-year-old *marché aux fleurs*, the sort of setting that brings to mind Madame Bovary. A delicious cloud of freesia, jasmine, and tuberose wafts across these Belle Époque halls—except on Sunday, when blossoms give way to beaks at the *marché aux oiseaux* (bird market).

www.parisinfo.com

BLOEMENMARKT

Amsterdam, The Netherlands

Hugging an attractive stretch of the Singel canal, Amsterdam's "floating" Bloemenmarkt is an apparition of colors so crazy, it's no wonder the 19th-century merchants got tulip mania. The barge stalls overflow with popular varieties like Queen of the Night. Pick up a bag of bulbs or some clogs to take home.

www.amsterdamtourist.com

CAMPO DEI FIORE

Rome, Italy

Founded in the 15th century, this little produce market occupies a special place in Romans' hearts. The romance begins at dawn, when farmers wheel in nature's bounty. The flower stalls are the last to close; stick around until 1 p.m., when the vendors really get the gab and throw in an extra rose or two.

www.turismoroma.it

ADDERLEY STREET FLOWER MARKET

Cape Town, South Africa

The country's largest flower hall market is renowned for the barbed wit of its female vendors, some of whom have been snipping and grinning here for decades. Prepare to shake, haggle, and roll away with heaps of carnations, lilies, and a lovely pincushion proteas, a native of South Africa.

tourismcapetown.co.za

PHOOL MANDI

New Delhi, India

Blooms plucked across the globe pop up at the *phool mandi*, one of Asia's most spectacular and bustling flower markets. It's wholesale, meaning the fragrant piles of *rajnigandha* (tuberoses), chrysanthemums, and lilies are bigger than usual. Bright orange marigolds, a favorite for traditional garlands, are sold from burlap bags the size of ottomans. Vendors start at dawn but vanish by 9 a.m.

www.delhitourism.gov.in

PAK KHLONG TALAT

Bangkok, Thailand

The Pak Khlong flower market is one of Bangkok's most nimble and arresting sights. Open around the clock, the stands are best enjoyed in the cool air after midnight, when boats on the Chao Phraya River deliver lotus blossoms in electrifying pink and white.

www.bangkoktourist.com

CAOJIADU

Shanghai, China

A vine-encrusted arch heralds the entrance to Caojiadu, the largest and busiest of Shanghai's flower markets. Spread over three floors, the sheer variety of plants and greenery can overwhelm anyone's Zen, although everyone agrees the prices are heavenly. There's enough here to equip a minibiosphere—birds, fish, turtles, and gurgling fountains.

www.meet-in-shanghai.net

DANGWA FLOWER MARKET

Manila, The Philippines

If love is in the air, pick up a bouquet from Dangwa—round about midnight. On Valentine's Day, crowds of Manila residents will be doing the very same thing. Stuffed into four lanes in the student quarter of Sampaloc, the stalls never think about closing; the bouquets are freshest when the barflies wilt.

www.manila.gov.ph

FLEMINGTON FLOWER MARKET

Sydney, Australia

Sydney's best kept secret is its cavernous flower market, achingly beautiful and buzzing from 5 a.m. with green energy. By about 9 a.m., the hustle fades as florists make off with their day's booty.

www.sydney.com

Two symbols of Amsterdam: A bicyclist stops to admire (and, perhaps, buy) some blooms at the city's flower market, Bloemenmarkt.

MEXICO

TEOTIHUACAN

Renew the spirit with the multitudes who gather each March to watch the sun rise over ancient ruins.

Thousands gather atop the Pyramid of the Sun on March 20, awaiting daybreak at Teotihuacan, the ancient ruins on the northern outskirts of Mexico City. Many are clad in white; some have brought crystals and amulets to capture the energy of the rising sun. When the orb finally appears over the Sierra Madre, people start to chant, sing, and pray, raising their arms to welcome the spring equinox.

Visitors will find the experience indelible. Explains Kenneth Fagan, who filmed the rites for Arizona State University, "It's very impressive to see nearly one million people in one location, mostly all in white, laughing, talking, singing, banging drums, dancing, playing flutes, and making animal sounds—people young and old, walking and climbing all over the ruins." For Mexicans, the celebration "connects them to their past, their history, and their family," Fagan says.

The "love-in" ambience invites everyone to participate. Join Aztec dancers and other troupes from all around Mexico. Munch freshly made tamales or bargain for trinkets with the many wandering vendors. Inhale the heady aroma of the copal incense burned by those who still believe in the ancient gods. Get your fortune told by a shaman. And have evil spirits exorcized by *brujos* (witches), on hand just in case the future doesn't look bright.

PLANNING Teotihuacan www.visitmexico.com. A good source of information on the ancient city is Arizona State University's Teotihuacan website, archaeology.asu.edu/teo.

IN THE KNOW
Pyramid of the Sun

Soaring 20 stories above the ancient city of Teotihuacan, the Pyramid of the Sun is the world's third largest pyramid and an iconic Mesoamerican structure. Construction began roughly 2,000 years ago. The pyramid's footprint is thought to be determined by the position of the setting sun on the spring and fall equinoxes. The adobe, stone, and plaster pyramid contains about 2.5 million tons (2.26 million tonnes) of rubble. No chambers have been found inside, but underneath is a mysterious lava-tube cave that may have been a religious shrine or royal tomb. Reach the flat summit by climbing its 248 steps.

Musicians dressed in traditional Indian costume are among those who gather at the Teotihuacan ruins to celebrate spring's arrival.

A woman in Guayaquil, Ecuador, sorts cacao beans destined for chocolatemaking abroad.

ECUADOR

See—and savor—fine chocolate during cacao's spring harvest in the botanical birthplace of the ancient elixir.

Cacao is harvested year-round all over Ecuador, but to indulge in the ultimate chocolate fantasy, head to the plantations in the tropical, Kichwa-speaking Amazon province of Napo. The region's chocolate recently made news when a special variety, Nacional, was found. The rare bean, once thought extinct, is considered the finest expression of cacao in the world.

Harvest in these parts begins in March, the first of two rainy seasons—but also the best time to experience the working side of the cacao production process when the drying, fermentation, and roasting occurs at the hands of small family farmers who've handed down harvest secrets over the generations. It's also the best time to witness the region's neon butterflies and intricately bejeweled hummingbirds for which this biodiverse hotspot—home to more than 4,000 plants, 1,000 birds, and 195 mammals—is known.

There are plenty of possibilities for exploring Ecuador's cacao farms, but the 850 family-run organic cocoa producers of the Kallari Association are especially worth seeking out. Each has earned kudos from Slow Food International for fair trade and sustainable agriculture practices, which help the local Kichwa people live without logging the rain forests.

PLANNING Ecuador www.ecuador.travel. Roast your own beans at the Chocolate Jungle plantation (*www.ecuadorjunglechocolate.com*), or ditch luxury for a chocolate volunteer vacation and Kichwa homestay at the Kallari Association (*kallari.com/internships.html*).

IN THE KNOW
A Cacao Love Affair

Though Venezuela claims the first cacao plants, Ecuador has played a starring role in the bean's rise. Today it is the world's largest producer of beans used to make fine chocolate. The country's Guayas Basin was home to the flavorful Arriba cacao bean, and new towns like Vinces in Los Ríos Province were founded on the wealth it brought to the region, where moneyed cacao barons settled. But a fungal outbreak in 1916–1919 ended the boom and decimated Ecuador's Arriba crops, and hardier, more disease-resistant varieties, like CCN-5, were planted instead.

GUATEMALA HIGHLANDS

"Ancient and wild, Guatemala stands out as an exciting destination for nature lovers. During spring's migration season, more than 720 kinds of birds can be found, each bursting with its own mix of colors. Twenty-two of these species, though rarely seen, are entirely endemic to the Guatemala Highlands, a land of bubbling volcanoes and ancient Quechan villages along ruin-lined Lake Atitlán."

—ADAM GRAHAM, NATIONAL GEOGRAPHIC WRITER

Commonly referred to as Los Altos by the locals, the Guatemalan Highlands is an upland region in the southern part of the country. The diverse physical landscape of volcanoes, canyons, and mountains is also home to rich Maya culture. *Pictured:* Hiking Volcán Pacaya, an active volcano

GRAND ST. PATRICK'S DAY CELEBRATIONS

Get your high-steppin' Irish on from Southie to the Costa Blanca.

NEW YORK CITY, NEW YORK

The granddaddy of all St. Patrick's Day parades (the first was staged in 1762 by homesick Irishmen serving in the British army) is also the world's largest, attracting more than two million spectators annually. Led by a military unit, the foot-powered procession (no cars or floats allowed) begins at 44th Street and marches on up Fifth Avenue for nearly six hours.

www.saintpatricksdayparade.com/nyc/newyorkcity.htm

BOSTON, MASSACHUSETTS

In the nation's most Irish state (nearly a quarter of Massachusetts' residents claim Irish ancestry), South Boston is St. Patrick's Day central. Since 1901, "Southie" has hosted the city's colossal parade (held on the Sunday closest to March 17) as thousands of marchers and revelers celebrate all things Emerald. Listen for the mournful wail of bagpipes calling marchers to the Broadway T station starting point.

www.southbostonparade.org

CHICAGO, ILLINOIS

Parade day (always a Saturday) begins with a wee bit of Irish magic (and 40 lb/18 kg of EPA-approved dye) to color the downtown Chicago River the perfect Kelly green. The St. Patrick's procession begins at noon, with bagpipers, horses, and high-stepping colleens leading the way north on Columbus Drive through Grant Park.

www.chicagostpatsparade.com

SAVANNAH, GEORGIA

Georgia's first city has been hosting a St. Patrick's Day parade since 1813. It's a three-hour rolling street party held on March 17 (a day earlier if the 17th falls on a Sunday). Book several months in advance to score a Historic District hotel room facing the parade route.

www.savannahsaintpatricksday.com

MONTSERRAT, WEST INDIES

The first Irish on this "Emerald Isle of the Caribbean" were former indentured servants fleeing religious persecution from neighboring islands in the 1600s. Shamrock passport stamps pay tribute to Montserrat's Hibernian roots, celebrated to a calypso beat during a weeklong St. Patrick's Festival. The Afro-Irish event also commemorates an attempted slave revolt on March 17, 1768.

www.visitmontserrat.com/St_Patricks_Festival

MONTREAL, QUEBEC, CANADA

Neither rain nor snow has ever canceled the Montreal St. Patrick's Parade. Run consecutively since 1824, the three-hour cavalcade of floats, bands, and costumed characters is traditionally held on the Sunday closest to March 17. Post-parade, the party continues at McKibbin's, Hurley's, the Sir Winston Churchill Complexe, and other downtown pubs.

www.montrealirishparade.com

DUBLIN, IRELAND

Dublin's St. Patrick's Festival is a four-day celebration of Irish culture and *craic* (good fun). The signature March 17 parade kicks off at noon from Parnell Square, continuing past Trinity College to the end point near St. Patrick's Cathedral. A half million revelers line the 1.6-mile (2.7 km) route, so for a view other than the back of someone's head, splurge for reserved grandstand seating.

www.stpatricksfestival.ie

BIRMINGHAM, ENGLAND

On the Sunday closest to St. Patrick's Day, the United Kingdom's largest St. Patrick's parade hums and high-steps through Digbeth, Birmingham's postindustrial Irish Quarter. Packed pubs line the route and the dress code trends emerald green, but the passing floats, dancers, and drum corps increasingly reflect the city's cultural diversity.

stpatricksbirmingham.com

CABO ROIG, SPAIN

Irish holidaymaker hot spot Cabo Roig hosts Spain's biggest St. Patrick's Day parade. Spend the morning at one of the town's white-sand Mediterranean beaches, and then snag a café table along the strip to cheer on the passing marching bands, motorbikes, and Irish dignitaries. A Guinness-fueled fiesta continues under the stars with karaoke, contests, fireworks, flamenco dancers, and more.

www.spain-holiday.com/Cabo-Roig

AUCKLAND, NEW ZEALAND

New Zealand's largest city hosts the world's first St. Patrick's Day party each year. Since Ireland-to-Auckland emigration began in the 1840s and continues today, there's palpable pride in the city's Irish heritage. Celebrations include a parade, a *fleadh* (dance and music fest), and lighting the 1,076-foot (328 m) Sky Tower green.

www.stpatrick.co.nz

Bagpipers turn their art into a marathon event as they keep pace for the long walk up Fifth Avenue during New York City's St. Patrick's Day parade.

AMSTERDAM

Paint the town orange for King's Day, when the whole city turns out to toast the lord of the land.

Stepping into the living Vermeer that is Amsterdam, with its tableau of canals and tidy homes, is the ultimate Dutch treat. Each spring, that poetic image turns on its head when thousands of merrymakers descend for King's Day, the apex of the Dutch annual calendar, on April 27.

The holiday is a kooky and unlikely show of national pride. Otherwise staid citizens dye their hair orange, don silly costumes, and slurp orange drinks to honor the official birthday of young King Willem-Alexander, known as Queen's Day until his mother Beatrix stepped down in 2013. The frenzy clogs streets in the central canal districts, forcing trams to grind to a halt.

"It's absolute mayhem," says Kimberley Lewis, who runs Randy Roy's walking tours of the red-light district. "The old center turns into one gigantic party." Meanwhile, every square inch of available sidewalk becomes a *vrijmarkt,* an open-air market where any Tom, Dirk, and Antje can hawk a few attic treasures.

Once the party's over, experience Dutch riches of a natural kind at the kaleidoscopic spring flower show at Keukenhof Gardens, 40 minutes southwest of Amsterdam. Wander onto these onetime royal hunting grounds and marvel at the choreographed blazes of blossoms—including, of course, Holland's world-famous tulips—blanketing 80 jaw-dropping acres (32 ha).

PLANNING **King's Day Festival** www.koninginnedagamsterdam.nl/queensday.html. **Keukenhof Gardens** www.keukenhof.nl. Keukenhof Gardens is open from late March to May.

IN THE KNOW
Tulip Mania

In Amsterdam's flower markets, 20 euros (about $28) will get you a bag of premium bulbs with change left over. But in the 17th century, a speculative fever for exotic tulips pushed values to insane heights. The most precious varieties had frilly edges and streaked petals caused by a louse-borne viral infection. In early 1637, a single Semper Augustus bulb cost more than ten years' wages of a skilled craftsman. Within a matter of weeks, the market collapsed, sparking a wave of bankruptcies. And what of the Semper Augustus? The line died out, its vigor sapped by the very virus the merchants had nurtured.

All the world's an orange blaze—both from hair dye and, on the Amsterdam waterfront, life jackets—during the annual King's Day (formerly Queen's Day).

Dutch politicians and celebrities demonstrate proper herring-eating form at an alfresco seaside festival celebrating the return of their favorite catch.

THE NETHERLANDS

SCHEVENINGEN

Join a timeless Dutch bash celebrating fresh "silver from the sea" at this seaside resort.

Back in the 18th century, Dutch fishermen would raise their festive *vlaggetjes* (pennants) when setting out to catch the first herring of the season. While that tradition has faded, every June a huge crowd gathers in Scheveningen, a beach town near The Hague, to fete Vlaggetjesdag (Flag Day). The harbor district quakes with marching bands, demonstrations of old crafts, and other traditional events. Fishing boats don their finest regalia, while ships of the Dutch Royal Navy lower their gangplanks to visitors.

On the Thursday before Flag Day, the first barrel of Hollandse Nieuwe, fresh young herring, is auctioned off for charity. Fat content is key: The minimum is 16 percent, and a really fine specimen has around 20 percent. The season lasts just six weeks, with the remaining catch frozen to be enjoyed at a later date. "Some fishmongers call it *nieuwe* the entire year," observes Frank Heyn, owner of Frank's Smokehouse in Amsterdam. "But a few months after the auction, it has lost its pizzazz."

At bustling harbor stalls, staggering numbers of plump filets are gobbled down with raw onions and pickles and chased with shots of *korenwijn*, a Dutch gin. The proper technique? Hold the herring aloft by the tail, and bite upward.

PLANNING Scheveningen www.scheveningendenhaag.com, www.denhaag.nl. Dates for the Hollandse Nieuwe auction and festivities may change on short notice. For background on Flag Day, see www.vlaggetjesdag.com.

BEST OF THE BEST
Mauritshuis in The Hague

The coastal scene at Scheveningen will have added meaning after a visit to the Mauritshuis museum in The Hague. Among the trove of 17th-century Golden Age masterworks is Johannes Lingelbach's "Departure of King Charles II from Scheveningen for England." The extensive collection of Dutch and Flemish paintings is spread over 16 rooms of this majestic, beautifully symmetrical 17th-century mansion overlooking the Hofvijver (Court Pond). Among its other highlights: Rembrandt's "Anatomy Lesson of Dr. Nicolaes Tulp" and Johannes Vermeer's "Girl With a Pearl Earring." (Due to renovations, select paintings will move to the Gemeentemuseum through mid-2014; others will be on tour.) www.mauritshuis.nl

Their name may be the "common starling," but there's nothing ordinary about the sight of a million starlings flying against a sunset backdrop.

DENMARK

WADDEN SEA NATIONAL PARK

Witness one of nature's most kinetic phenomena when waves of starlings form in the springtime skies.

A tangle of salty, squelching reed beds on the western coast of Denmark, wafer-thin Wadden Sea National Park—the country's largest nature reserve—is perfectly placed on a migratory superhighway. For bird-watchers, the prime slot is mid-March to April, when the tall, woody grasses turn a beautiful, tender green, just in time for a mesmerizing aerial ballet known as the *sort sol,* or "black sun."

The spectacle occurs at dusk, when swarms of more than a million starlings erupt from their feeding grounds and etch amazing patterns into a darkening sky. Hawks, eagles, and other birds of prey on the hunt prompt the starlings to take on especially dramatic, ever-changing formations—a beautiful but potentially deadly show.

The best place to go is the coastal Tønder Marsh in southern Jutland, not far from the German border. While pinpoint accuracy isn't possible, a savvy tour guide can narrow the odds of spotting the flocks. "We have people in the field who find the starlings ahead of time," says Iver Gram, owner of Dansk Natursafari, which leads 25,000 visitors into the UNESCO-listed region every year. "Then we crouch in the reeds around sunset to watch and wait."

PLANNING Denmark www.visitdenmark.com. **Wadden Sea Center and starling tours** www.vadehavs centret.dk. **Danish national parks** www.danmarksnationalparker.dk.

BEST OF THE BEST
Møgeltønder Church

While waiting for dusk and the starlings to dance, pay a visit to Møgeltønder, a well-scrubbed hamlet about 5 miles (8 km) from Tønder Marsh. The town's 13th-century Møgeltønder Church boasts one of Denmark's most lavish interiors. In the beautiful Romanesque nave, a creaking wooden ceiling is the canvas for biblical events framed in billowing clouds, while the elaborate four-winged altar (ca 1500) shines with gilt detail. Amid the riches, a sly wit emerges: The carved pulpit is held aloft by cherubs, while impish faces peer from pipes on the organ, the country's oldest.

MONTE-CARLO

Rub elbows with *tout le monde* at the weeklong Grand Prix, when speed and glamour mix along the French Riviera.

I t's not the screaming metal demons that make the Monaco Grand Prix such a singular motor-racing experience; it's the ability of mere mortals to walk the track—and perhaps mingle casually with the world's greatest drivers—just hours before and after the furious Formula One action each May.

The whole of race week in the tiny principality is that way. You might find yourself sitting next to racing champ Sebastian Vettel at the trackside Chez Bacco restaurant or sharing elbow room at the bar with Will Smith in the posh La Rascasse nightclub, a darling with drivers and celebrities who populate the annual race turned see-and-be-seen event.

Duane Penner, who arranges customized Grand Prix trips, calls it a "truly iconic event." He elaborates: "It's got royalty and beautiful people parties. It takes place on the French Riviera. It's got Ferrari and Mercedes-Benz. Just walking around you feel like you're part of something."

Get a feel for the 2.1-mile (3.3 km) course by walking or biking the sinuous street circuit on one of those blue-sky spring days that add to Monte-Carlo's glitter. And watch Sunday's race from a private terrace perched high above the track—sipping Dom Pérignon, of course, because during race week in Monaco, only the best will do.

PLANNING Monaco www.visitmonaco.com. Customized tours of the Grand Prix *(www.roadtrips.com)* include private party invitations, helicopter transfers to and from Nice Airport, and race viewing from a private balcony at the Hôtel de Paris.

IN THE KNOW
Europe's Other Great Races

● **ISLE OF MAN TT:** Since 1907, public highways have been used for this hard-core spring motorcycle event on this island in the Irish Sea. Racers reach speeds exceeding 130 mph (210 kph) on the 38-mile (61 km) circuit. www.iomtt.com

● **LE MANS:** First held in 1923, Le Mans is the world's oldest and most prestigious endurance race, lasting 24 hours. High-performance cars compete on an 8.5-mile (13.7 km) circuit in western France. www.lemans.org

● **RALLY FINLAND:** Raced in Jyväskylä on gravel roads in souped-up versions of ordinary street cars, Scandinavia's top auto race spans three days in late July or early August. The course is known for its high-speed turns and big air jumps. www.nesteoilrallyfinland.fi

City driving takes on a whole new meaning as the Monaco Grand Prix roars around Monte-Carlo's narrow streets.

One of Paris's 37 spans across the Seine, the Alexander III Bridge commemorates friendship between Russia and France.

FRANCE
PARIS

Renew your spirit with the city's irresistible spring display—in gardens, restaurants, and cafés and on the court.

P aris radiates a special glow in spring, when flowers decorate the streets and parks, people-watchers luxuriate in sidewalk cafés, restaurant menus take on a lighter touch, and the season seems to actually sing—with an utterly Parisian accent.

To appreciate the best of the season, take to the streets. As you promenade from one *quartier* to the next, you'll admire clouds of fragrant color—daffodils, tulips, hyacinths, wisteria, lilacs, roses, peonies—framing ancient arches, columns, and stone walls. "Strolling the city's parks and streetlets when the almond trees pop into minty bloom, you feel like you've wandered into a Jean-Jacques Sempé illustration," says *National Geographic Traveler* magazine writer Olivia Stren, who has visited family in Paris all her life.

One favorite floral spot is little Square Vert Gallant near Pont Neuf, where manicured flower beds decorate a Parisian scene of plane trees and grass-framed promenades surrounded by the Seine. Another is the Musée Rodin's spectacularly fragrant rose garden (where picnics are allowed).

For something even more special, head to one of the city's many painstakingly maintained parks and gardens. Whispers of France's departed royals linger in the Left Bank's Jardin du

As you promenade from one quartier to the next, you'll admire clouds of fragrant color— daffodils, tulips, hyacinths, wisteria, lilacs, roses, peonies —framing ancient arches, columns, and stone walls.

The Eiffel Tower is an amazing site any time of year, but in spring, flowers are painstakingly groomed around its base to add a photogenic touch.

While away the hours at Les Deux Magots discussing the works of former regulars Hemingway and Sartre—or give over to people-watching.

Luxembourg, where you'll find statue-dotted formal gardens and an orchard filled with apple and pear trees glorious in their peak bloom. Relatively unknown, the Parc Floral de Paris is a gorgeous botanical garden in the Bois de Vincennes, showcasing 3,000 manicured plant varieties from around the world, including magnificent roses; stroll its grassy paths, then settle down in an Impressionist landscape to enjoy a *pique-nique* in the sun. And don't miss the Promenade Plantée, a defunct elevated railway line beginning near the Bastille where springtime cherry trees, chestnut trees, and colorful flower gardens accent an afternoon stroll.

To bring some blooms home (or at least to your hotel room), visit one of the many flower vendors along the Seine, perhaps Marché d'Aligre on the Place d'Aligre, Cler Fleurs *(46 Rue Cler),* or the picturesque Marché aux Fleurs near Notre-Dame (a flower market that on Sundays switches to a sweet-sounding bird market).

SPOTS FOR A PERFECT PICNIC

A picnic in Paris in springtime is a must. Be authentically Parisian in the huge Bois de Boulogne, on the western edge of the 16th Arrondissement: Rent a boat and explore the islets dotting the lake. Commissioned by Emperor Napoleon III, the Parc des Buttes Chaumont is a hilly landscape, with trails and winding pathways, located in the 19th Arrondissement. And the famed Jardin des Tuileries outside the Louvre is replete with a series of graceful sculptures, fascinating bronze works, and wonderful urban views. Don't forget to bring a bottle of wine. Three wonderful selections for the season: a sparkling Tissot Crémant du Jura rosé; a 2010 Domaine du Bagnol cassis, another rosé; or a 2009 cabernet, Gauthier Bourgueil Soif de Jour. These wines go with any food. *Santé!*

THE CAFÉ SCENE

When all is said and done, there's no better way to celebrate the end of the winter doldrums than at an outdoor café—take a book, order a coffee, and bask beneath the bright blue sky. You'll find suitable cafés throughout the city; for some of its most famous, head to the Carrefour Vavin (renamed Place Pablo Picasso) and seek out Le Select, Le Dôme, La Rotonde, La Coupole, or even the Dingo American Bar, where in April 1925 Ernest Hemingway introduced himself to F. Scott Fitzgerald.

In this city of gourmands, Parisian restaurants update their menus with the season's finest ingredients—including spring lamb, plump strawberries, bright green beans, white asparagus, morel mushrooms, spring chèvre, and daily catches of John Dory, cod, and turbot. You can enjoy a chef's take on the season or peruse a farmers' market for your own feast. Julia Child frequented the market on Rue Cler; other excellent markets include Bastille and Place Monge.

PLANNING **Paris** www.viator.com. **Guided tours** www.toursbylocals.com. **Food and wine** www.foodandwine.com, www.eatinparis.com, www.localwineevents.com.

IN THE KNOW
The City's Sporting Side

Spring also offers less reflective action—and great outdoor spectator sports: Tennis's French Open starts in May at Stade Roland-Garros *(www.roland garros.com).* There's horse racing at the Hippodrome d'Auteuil and Hippodrome de Longchamp (both *en.parisinfo.com).* Paris Saint-Germain's soccer season is also in full swing, its home games played at Parc des Princes stadium *(www.psg.fr).* Or, sit back and watch a traditional boules match in the Luxembourg Gardens or in one of the small parks along the boulevards.

Champions often take flight at the French Open, aka Roland-Garros, named for an early French aviator.

Top 10

SPRING VINEYARDS

Savor the pleasures that come with a spring visit to these outstanding wineries.

INNISKILLIN WINES

Niagara-on-the-Lake, Ontario, Canada

Canada is the epicenter of ice wine, which is made from grapes harvested in subfreezing temperatures, which concentrates their flavor, complexity, and sugars. Inniskillin helped pioneer the process in Canada, and its tastings show surprising range. Its on-site restaurant pairs food expertly.

inniskillin.com

PENNER-ASH WINE CELLARS

Newberg, Oregon

Oregon's Willamette Valley has become one of the world's celebrated wine destinations. The reason: Pinot Noir. While you'll find dozens of notable producers, Penner-Ash Wine Cellars may be one of the prettiest (and friendliest). With bands of windows and a floating roofline, the tasting room and its views are as memorable as the wines.

www.pennerash.com

JUSTIN VINEYARDS AND WINERY

Paso Robles, California

Even beer drinkers know that Napa and Sonoma produce great wines, but recently attention has turned south. Paso Robles on California's Central Coast produces rich reds, including Cabernet Sauvignon and Syrah. At Justin Vineyards and Winery, you'll find a striking Tuscan-style tasting room, restaurant, and B&B, along with its Cabernet-based Isosceles blend.

www.justinwine.com

PEDERNALES CELLARS

Stonewall, Texas

The Texas Hill Country, with its rolling countryside and spring-fed rivers, once evoked images of the Wild West. But now it has vineyards, too, and Pedernales Cellars offers one of the prettiest places to take it all in. Come at sunset to sip award-winning Viogniers and Tempranillos. John Wayne never had it this good.

pedernalescellars.com

LAURA HARTWIG

Santa Cruz, Chile

About two hours south of Santiago, vineyards crowd the compact Colchagua Valley between the Andes and the Pacific. By all means, taste the Carménère, Chile's signature grape long misidentified as Merlot. At the boutique winery Laura Hartwig, visitors pass polo fields and tennis courts before arriving at a traditional-style bodega.

CAVAS RECAREDO

Sant Sadurní d'Anoia, Spain

Spain calls its sparkling wine Cava because the French have claim to the more familiar name Champagne. But the bubbly produced in the Penedès region south of Barcelona is just as festive. Unlike the area's industrial-scale wineries, Cavas Recaredo still produces by hand and uses Earth-friendly biodynamic methods.

recaredo.es

DOMAINE DU DALEY

Lutry, Switzerland

You'll marvel at the Lake Geneva view, but don't forget the vineyard. Swiss wines are often overlooked because the country keeps most to itself and exports very little. Domaine du Daley, which dates from 1392, grows 12 grape varieties. Make sure to sip the Chasselas, a dry, fruity wine perfect with raclette cheese.

www.daley.ch

VECCHIE TERRE DI MONTEFILI

Greve in Chianti, Italy

"Super Tuscan" sounds like a comic book hero, but it's a type of Italian wine that once flaunted the regulations governing blends and labeling. Sample some at family-run Vecchie Terre di Montefili, south of Florence. In addition to the super Tuscans, try the Chianti Classico—it's a pure 100 percent Sangiovese, instead of a blend.

vecchieterredimontefili.it/eng

CRAMELE RECAS

Recas, Romania

The Roman god Bacchus supposedly came from Romania, and even now Cramele Recas, among the hillside vineyards in the Transylvania region, produces surprisingly good but inexpensive Cabernet Sauvignons and white blends. And its vampire and werewolf labels are just fun.

www.recaswine.ro

SERESIN ESTATE

Renwick, Marlborough, New Zealand

Sauvignon Blanc put New Zealand on the wine map—and gave visitors another reason to visit the country's scenic South Island. At Seresin, grapes grow without pesticides and are harvested by hand. The vineyard offers tastings at outdoor tables among the vines and a chance to sample the internationally trained winemaker's olive oil as well.

seresin.co.nz

Switzerland's Dézaley wine region, planted since the 12th century, overlooks Lake Geneva from breathtakingly steep cliffs.

With banners aloft and their faith strong, Romanies honor St. Sara, who is said to have arrived on these shores by boat.

FRANCE

SAINTES-MARIES-DE-LA-MER

Join a colorful springtime celebration of ancient miracles as the region rejoices with a colorful Romany pilgrimage.

A marshland frontier that lies in France's Provence region between the ancient city of Arles and the Mediterranean, the Camargue is famed for its long-horned bulls and magnificent white horses with flowing manes. A supreme bird reserve, it's home to nearly 300 species, the most famous denizen probably being the great flamingo. To watch these lanky pink birds gliding effortlessly in the pure blue sky is one of Provence's most memorable sites.

AN ANCIENT LEGEND

The landscape's quiet mood changes dramatically in spring. On May 24 and 25 every year, bedecked in colorful skirts and scarves with the jingling of silver jewelry filling the air, thousands of Romanies flock here for baptisms, family reunions, and to pay homage to their revered St. Sara, the Egyptian servant girl who accompanied a boatful of early Christians here around A.D. 40.

Legend has it that soon after Jesus Christ was crucified, three Marys—Mary Magdalene; Mary Jacobé, the Virgin Mary's sister; and Mary Salomé, mother of the Apostles James and John—along with their servant Sara, were shoved out to sea without sails or oars. They

IN THE KNOW
Bull Games

Throughout the Camargue in summer, the region's semiwild long-horned bulls are rounded up, destined for the bullring. In the *courses camarguaises*, as the bullfights are called, the bull is never killed. Instead, the events are a thrilling cat-and-mouse game between the bull and *raseteurs*, who attempt to unhook strings and tassels from the animal's horns with handheld rakes. Points are awarded for retrieving different items. The crowd erupts in screams and shouts as the men egg on the bull, trying to make him charge. The most prestigious games—July's Cocarde d'Or—occur in Arles, with others taking place in Nîmes, Tarascon, and Saintes-Maries-de-la-Mer.

drifted and finally washed ashore here, where the settlement became known as Saintes-Maries-de-la-Mer ("Saint Marys of the Sea"). The grateful Marys built a chapel, where the relics of Mary Salomé and Mary Jacobé are said to be preserved. Beside them stands a statue of their honorary saint Sara, covered with a huge layer of dresses provided as offerings.

PROCESSION TO THE SEA

On May 24, Romany pilgrims partake in a Catholic Mass inside the Église des Saintes-Maries, followed by a grand, cacophonous procession that transports Sara's statue from the church to the sea, escorted by elegant white Camargue horses. The pilgrims strain to touch and kiss the statue, believing they will receive health-giving properties in return. "Being there was magic," says Delazad Deghati, a film student who has spent time shooting the festival. "All these people, most of whose lives are not easy, were enjoying themselves immensely. Colors, dresses—everything—was warm and happy."

The statue is bathed in the sea as pilgrims dance and throw flowers to bless the water. The singing crowd then accompanies Sara back to the church amid cheers and the peal of church bells. The festivities continue late into the evening, with the procession repeating itself the next day. "To be a part of this celebration made me nearly cry from happiness," Deghati says.

PLANNING Saintes-Maries-de-la-Mer www.saintesmaries.com. **Provence** www.beyond.fr. The ancient city of Arles, 45 minutes north, has many options for lodging (*www.avignon-et-provence.com*).

GREAT STAYS
The Camargue

● **L'AUBERGE CAVALIÈRE DU PONT DES BANNES:** Individual lodges constructed with traditional adobe walls and thatched roofs. Inside, though, are handsome, modern interiors. www.auberge cavaliere.com

● **MAS DE LA FOUQUE:** A traditional Camargue hotel, with large rooms, tiled floors, and wooden beams. Private terraces overlook the lagoon and park. www.masdelafouque.com

● **MAS DE PEINT:** A working ranch in the center of the Camargue, offering horseback rides through the wild countryside, this farmstead is a remarkable combination of elegance and authenticity. www.masdepeint.com

In a land that's also home to hundreds of varieties of birds, pilgrims pay homage at the Church of Saintes-Maries-de-la-Mer.

The terraced gardens fronting Lake Como at Villa Monastero showcase sculpture-ornamented promenades and a collection of citrus trees.

ITALY

LAKE COMO

Surround yourself with the sweet, spring-scented life amid grand villas and perfectly tended gardens.

From the water at night, the lake seems to have stepped out of time. The mansions along the shore cast their lights, glittering like stars in the ferry's wake. The faint tinkle of fine stemware and laughter spills out an open hotel window, patios full of people shaking off winter like they've just come out of hibernation.

Como, about 30 miles (48 km) long, is Europe's deepest lake, dropping more than 1,300 feet (410 m). But it's a lake to be on, not in—a famous actor's house swallowed up the one good public beach—and the water has paid the price for the region's industry and agricultural runoff. Still, that's meant nothing to the views: Ripening vineyards stretch up the hills, and each lakefront house looks like it's simply waiting for the return of a slower, quieter time when servants were cheap and cocktail hour went on all through the long spring twilight, scented by countless blossoms.

Comfortable, efficient ferries connect every section of the lake, and that's the best way to see Lake Como; yes, there's a road, but it's more an apology than a good way to get around. From the water, Como best reveals its secrets: Villas hidden from land by trees and vines show their secret faces over fresh lawns; hotels that have hosted royalty and rock stars, honeymoons and golden anniversaries; glimpses of gardens in new spring bloom; fountains

From the water at night, the lake seems to have stepped out of time. The mansions along the shore cast their lights, glittering like stars in the ferry's wake.

One area, an endless supply
of gifts: Varenna's lake views,
spring produce, and a general
understanding that, here,
there is no reason to rush

Perched on the
edge of Lake Como,
Varenna's winding
lanes and rustic
fishermen's houses
have views to the
Italian Alps.

unleashed from winter's freeze; and artwork through loggias. The warming spring air is like a caress from the water, as the lake again invites exploration.

INDULGE ALONG COBBLESTONE STREETS

On the south-central shore, nestled on the peninsula where the lake splits like a "Y," lies Bellagio, a small village of twisted cobblestone streets and stairways hiding pastry and gelato shops that seem to appear like welcome buds among the high-fashion boutiques. The gray stones of the 12th-century Church of San Giacomo peer over blazing white luxe hotels down toward the lake's smooth, blue water. Restaurants fight for attention with the spring's first produce, and around it all, villas show what a couple hundred years of paying attention to the gardens can do with hillsides, now solid colors. No view ever seems to appear twice, as if each corner brings a new lake into being. The town has been famous as a resort since Roman times. After a walking tour or an afternoon strolling its charming, winding streets, it will be easy to see why the town's nickname is the "Pearl of the Lake."

TAKE IN THE VIEWS

Bellagio isn't the only town on the lake; the city of Como still has its ancient walls and a town center as twisted as a maze. There, you can catch a funicular and ride up into the Alps to Brunate, almost a half mile (0.8 km) above the lake, for a view of scenery clear to Switzerland. Heartier souls can take one of the hiking trails on the edge of town, catching the last patches of snow in shadowed groves. Como's also famous for silk, with a museum that shows what Marco Polo was after in China, and shops where the silk patterns form their own gardens of color.

LIVE VICARIOUSLY: THE HEIGHT OF LUXURY

But maybe the best thing to do on Lake Como is simply see what it was like when the living was easy. Check out the mansions, grand villas surrounded by landscape that looks like it's been tended by tweezers and tiny scissors, the fragrant blossoms of *gelsomino* (jasmine) climbing walls like ivy. The 17th-century Villa Carlotta has an expanse of perfect, perfumed gardens, where the season's dazzling rhododendrons, azaleas, and an array of rare plants will be showing off now. The Villa del Balbianello started as a Franciscan monastery, was turned into a luxury home in the late 18th century, and ended up as the backdrop in a *Star Wars* movie.

That's Lake Como in the spring: anything you dream, surrounded by flowers.

PLANNING **Lake Como** www.discovercomo .com. **Ferry service** www.navigazionelaghi .it. **Bellagio** www.bellagiolakecomo.com. **Villa Carlotta** www.villacarlotta.it. **Villa del Balbianello** villabalbianello.com. The area is best reached by train from Milan (*www.trenitalia.com*).

BEST OF THE BEST
The Island in the Lake

Come spring, when long winter shadows cast by the mountains have abated, Isola Comacina on Lake Como's western side is an ideal spot for the season's first picnic. Among the stones of ancient Roman ruins and shaded by olive trees, dine with a view of the sun as it moves across the Sacro Monte di Ossuccio, a 17th-century religious complex in the distance. Boats run from the local museum, the Antiquarium, to the tip of the island, like a ferry from one world to another. www.isola-comacina.it

Ancient busts at Villa Melzi in Bellagio encourage visitors to step outside into the sunshine.

GIRONA FLOWER FESTIVAL

"The medieval city of Girona overflows with creativity during its annual spring flower festival, the Temps de Flors. Surprising floral creations spill down cathedral steps and bloom-inspired art installations fill city squares and stone-walled courtyards."

—ABIGAIL KING, *NATIONAL GEOGRAPHIC TRAVELER* WRITER

The northeastern Spanish city of Girona transforms annually between May 7 and 15 into one enormous garden, covered with colorful floral arrangements for the Girona Flower Festival, known in Catalan as the Temps de Flors. *Pictured:* Floral artists put finishing touches to a festival street mural.

SINAI AWAKENING
Bruce Feiler
St. Catherine's Monastery

I bolted upright the first time I heard the bells. I held my ears when I realized the clamor was just outside my door. And when the ringing showed no signs of stopping, I stuffed my head back under the covers. A carillon 15 centuries old; a wake-up call older than the clock.

St. Catherine's Monastery, in the southern mountains of the Sinai Peninsula, was founded 1,500 years ago by monks who believed it was where Moses heard the voice of God. The dozen or so monks who still live there today hold services five times a day in Byzantine Greek.

The night before, I decided to go for a stroll in the dark. I tiptoed down a set of stairs, past a room that contains all the skulls of all the monks who've ever lived at the monastery. They spill out of a crypt like Cheerios onto the floor. At the end of the alley is a large, raspberry bramble about 10 feet (3 m) tall. The monks say this particular bush has been here since Moses passed by 3,200 years ago.

I sat down to reflect. With the light from gas lamps and the shadow of the mountain above that some believe is where Moses received the Ten Commandments, I felt a sense of awe. But then I noticed something by the base of the bush. It was a fire extinguisher. At first, I thought it was just an eyesore, and then I realized: Is this in case the burning bush catches on fire?! And if it does, should I put it out or look for the face of God?

I tried to put the image out of my mind, but then a white cat with a brown patch over its eye jumped out of the bush, landed at my feet, and screeched. I ran back to my room to brush up on my Byzantine Greek.

Spring is Passover, when the Israelites are said to have left Egypt and walked this route. Spring is Easter, filled with symbols of renewal. In almost 20 years visiting sacred sites around the world, I find St. Catherine's the holiest place I've ever been. It defies centuries. It houses an impressive cross-section of different architectural and religious traditions. And to me, it defines spring.

Bruce Feiler (www.brucefeiler.com) *is the author of the international best-seller* Walking the Bible *and host of the PBS series* Walking the Bible *and the forthcoming* Sacred Journeys with Bruce Feiler. *His latest book is* The Secrets of Happy Families.

"In almost 20 years visiting sacred sites around the world, I find St. Catherine's the holiest place I've ever been."

In the stone kitchen of St. Catherine's, priests and Bedouins gather to shape bread dough into loaves.

MOROCCO

FEZ

Take in far-flung sounds in Morocco's spiritual and cultural capital.

Twelve-hundred-year-old Fez, Morocco's intellectual, artistic, and spiritual heart, has forever beguiled with its collision of the medieval and the modern (this is the sort of place where you'll find mule-cart drivers busy texting on their mobiles). The weeklong Festival of World Sacred Music, like Fez itself, also enchants with its colorful contrasts. The summertime event woos visitors with its musical rencontres, collaborations between artists hailing from wildly diverging cultures and traditions—such diverse talents as Icelandic rock star Bjork, American folk legend Joan Baez, and Congolese-French rapper Abd al Malik.

In the daytime, find cool reprieve from the city's sun-torched summer streets in the Andalusian gardens of the Musée Batha, a 19th-century sultanate palace. Here, afternoon recitals—where you might hear *qanun*-accompanied Aramaic songs, the sounds of Tuareg nomad groups, Koranic phrases set to gospel harmonies, Senegalese *mbalax* rhythms, or Blue Note–style jazz—are set to storybook effect under the shade of an enormous Barbary oak tree. Post concert, wander through the museum, now home to a formidable collection of Fassi embroidery and 14th-century ceramics. By night, head to the Bab al Makina, the gold-plated gates of the Royal Palace. Grand and moonlit, the palace doors serve as romantic and moody backdrop to the festival's nighttime concerts.

PLANNING Fez Festival of World Sacred Music www.fesfestival.com

GREAT STAYS
La Maison Bleue

Festivalgoers who spent the evening at the threshold of a palace can also bid *bonne nuit* in one. In the heart of the city's labyrinthine medina, the Maison Bleue is the lavish former home of renowned Moroccan judge, professor, and astrologer Sidi Mohammed El Abbadi (the place was restored by his grandchildren). If the palatial decor (blue *zellij* tile work, carved cedar doors, spouting fountains, canopy beds) pampers them, guests here can also indulge in history: A library houses antique bound books, texts, and oil paintings. www.maisonbleue.com

With hot pink lights setting off the night sky, the Belen Maya Spanish Dance Company takes to the stage at the Festival of World Sacred Music.

Hikers survey the scene from the peak of one of the Atlas Mountains in Imilchil, Morocco. Next stop, the 13,671-foot (4,167 m) peak of Jebel Toubkal?

MOROCCO

ATLAS MOUNTAINS

Explore the strongholds of Berber culture in the villages and valleys when the spring thaw clears the way.

B erbers proudly call themselves Imazighen, or free people. Meet these fiercely independent tribes in settlements tucked below one of the Atlas Mountains's highest peaks, Jebel Toubkal. Whether you plan a rigorous overnight hike to the top at 13,671 feet (4,167 m) or make a day trip from Marrakech to villages like Imlil, the spring thaw makes the season the most exhilarating time to visit. Melting snow rushes through the streams of the Ourika Valley and budding trees make an unforgettable contrast as you ascend from the arid landscape of the city. Overhead, massive cumulus clouds drift over the hills, alternating with brilliant sunlight.

Village life revolves around Islamic icons: the mosque, madrassa, bread oven, public fountain, and hammam, a communal steam bathhouse. Days are punctuated with chants echoing among the stone valleys of muezzins calling worshippers to prayer. And in this traditional culture, you will rarely glimpse a woman's tattooed face, a mark of her tribe; most stay far from sight.

"It's what I would call the real Morocco," says Mike McHugo, owner of Kasbah du Toubkal, an Imlil guesthouse. Be sure to pack an extra bag, along with your bargaining skills; you'll want to shop for brilliant, handwoven wool carpets.

PLANNING Atlas Mountains www.visitmorocco.com. Western High Atlas operators offer custom tours of the Toubkal National Park region by foot, mule, or camel. The area is an easy 37-mile (60 km) drive from Marrakech.

GREAT STAYS
Kasbah du Toubkal

A former mountain fortress, or casbah, the Kasbah du Toubkal offers modern, comfortable lodgings with unforgettable views of the High Atlas. Spring's longer, warmer days allow you to relax on its sunny terrace or to spend a day trekking rocky paths. In the evening, the Kasbah offers warming tagine stews and conversations with other travelers around a blazing fireplace. As you return to your en suite room, stop to appreciate the frosty night sky, studded with stars. The Kasbah devotes some of its profits to Education for All, a charity that supports secondary education for girls. www.kasbahdutoubkal.com

MAGNIFICENT GARDENS

Inhale spring's breathtaking perfume in extraordinary landscapes that range from vast to intimate.

BUTCHART GARDENS
Vancouver, Canada

This former limestone quarry was transformed into magnificent gardens in 1904. Located on Vancouver Island, its rolling landscape features more than a million bedding plants from 700 varieties for uninterrupted blooming from March through October. Wander through the Sunken Garden in the original quarry and the Japanese Garden facing Butchart Cove.
www.butchartgardens.com

BROOKLYN BOTANIC GARDENS
Brooklyn, New York

Founded in 1910, this sprawling garden in the heart of Brooklyn highlights more than 6,000 plant species. The Bonsai Museum showcases some 350 carefully sculpted trees, one of the largest collections on public display outside Japan. In late April, more than 45,000 bluebells burst into flower and picnickers gather beneath the Cherry Esplanade's blooming trees.
www.bbg.org

JARDIM BOTÂNICO DE CURITIBA
Curitiba, Brazil

Located in the capital of Brazil's southern Paraná state, these French-style botanical gardens center around a towering greenhouse reminiscent of London's 19th-century Crystal Palace. In the Garden of Sensations, visitors stroll blindfolded, experiencing the surrounding foliage and trickling waterfalls through sound, smell, and touch.
www.visitbrasil.com

KEUKENHOF GARDENS
Lisse, The Netherlands

With more than seven millions tulips, daffodils, and hyacinths in bloom from March to May, this 79-acre (32 ha) spread southwest of Amsterdam is considered the world's largest flower garden. View the tulip fields from "whisper boats," electric-powered boats that glide almost silently through the Dutch landscape.
www.keukenhof.nl

MONET'S GARDEN
Giverny, France

Many of Impressionist master Claude Monet's most famous paintings were inspired by the flower and water gardens he cultivated around his home northwest of Paris. Open from April to November, the gardens burst with narcissus, jonquils, and wisteria. Stroll around the pond in May, when sunlight and shadow play over Monet's beloved water lilies.
fondation-monet.com/en

VILLA D'ESTE
Tivoli, Italy

A Renaissance masterpiece of Italian gardening, this sprawling complex northeast of Rome features grottoes, waterfalls, and ancient statues. Explore the ruins of the Villa Adriana, built by the Roman emperor Hadrian, and the spouting animal heads and lilies along the Avenue of the Hundred Fountains.
www.villadestetivoli.info/storiae.htm

KIRSTENBOSCH
Cape Town, South Africa

Set against the eastern slopes of Cape Town's Table Mountain, this 89-acre (36 ha) garden was established in 1913 to conserve fynbos, southern Africa's unique plant life. Visit in the South African spring, between August and November, to view the fynbos at its best and see the greatest number of plants in flower.
www.sanbi.org/gardens/kirstenbosch

SEYCHELLES NATIONAL BOTANICAL GARDENS
Victoria, Seychelles

Established more than a century ago in the island nation's capital, the Botanical Gardens is one of the Seychelles's oldest national monuments. Look for native orchids, rare spice trees, roosting fruit bat colonies, and giant tortoises from Aldabra, some of which are more than 150 years old.
www.seychelles.travel

SINGAPORE BOTANIC GARDEN
Singapore

Founded in 1859, the Botanic Garden displays lush bougainvillea, bamboo, palm trees, and other native tropical plants over 128 acres (52 ha). Visit the Healing Garden for a peaceful walk among plants traditionally used in Southeast Asian medicine, then hike to the 7.5-acre (3 ha) National Orchid Garden at the park's highest point, where more than 60,000 orchids bloom.
www.sbg.org.sg

KENROKU-EN
Kanazawa, Japan

Developed by feudal lords in the 17th century, Kenroku-en is considered one of the most beautiful gardens in Japan. The strolling-style landscape features artfully designed ponds, hills, and teahouses. In March, hundreds of plum trees show off dark pink and white blossoms while irises flower along the garden's winding streams.
www.pref.ishikawa.jp

For more than a century, Butchart Gardens has offered residents and visitors of Vancouver Island 50-plus acres (20 ha) of tranquillity, beauty, and photo ops.

JAIPUR, INDIA

HOLI FESTIVAL
OF COLORS

"All along the roads the air is filled with singing and drum beating.
Everything is colored yellowish red and rendered dusty by the heaps of
scented powder blown all over."

—*RATNAVALI*, SEVENTH-CENTURY DRAMA

After the first full moon in March, Holi celebrations bring India to life, as people throw colored
powder to commemorate the coming of spring. The northern city of Jaipur enhances the celebrations further with its Elephant Festival.

Andrew Evans

May Days in Kiev

Cannon fire with a magnificent boom, followed by gentle white wisps of gun smoke that flutter skyward. The air is warm and the music loud—a military brass band marches the mile (1.6 km) of Khreshchatyk, and thundering drumbeats echo off the imposing gray facades that line Kiev's central boulevard.

The crowd swarms like honeybees, making way for the white-haired veterans who wear their polished medals with pride. Timid children in their best clothing hand pink carnations to the aging heroes. Over and over, I watch this touching gift between generations and I am moved.

Victory Day falls on May 9, a day to remember the end of the Great Patriotic War, World War II. Though families are here for the pony rides and hot dogs and Mylar balloons, the Ukrainian nation will never forget the time when Nazi armies marched down this same boulevard.

May is my favorite time in Ukraine's capital, when the long winter ends abruptly and the city stops to party for a good ten days. The fun begins on Labor Day, the first of May, when an old Soviet habit still grants all workers the day off. Though a few red stars still linger in the city, today's May Day is a joyous shout to the pagan rites of spring.

The snow is gone and in its place, the lacy white blossoms of chestnut trees cover the city's steep hills that slope down into the fast-flowing Dnieper. From this flowering forest poke the shiny golden domes of Kiev's Pechersk Lavra, a thousand-year-old Orthodox monastery built over a labyrinth of deep and natural caves.

Though this city is ancient, Ukraine is still a young country. The May holidays mark a youthful change of pace, leaving indoors for outdoors, moving from darkness into light. Each new day lasts a little longer. And, in the weeks that follow, the rich black earth will turn into brilliant green—in Ukrainian, the word for May is *traven,* or "grass."

All of this is cause for celebration—a reminder that no matter the upheaval of war, no matter how cold and terrible the winter, the rhythm of nature will continue, bringing new life each spring.

Andrew Evans is a contributing editor at National Geographic Traveler *magazine as well as National Geographic's "Digital Nomad," traveling the globe to create interactive travel experiences for readers. He is also the author of best-selling guidebooks to Ukraine and Iceland.*

"May is my favorite time in Ukraine's capital ... a joyous shout to the pagan rites of spring."

Founded during the early 12th century, Kiev's St. Michael's Cathedral—devoted to the city's patron saint—kicked off the trend of gilding domes.

OSAKA AND TOKYO

Experience the thunderously popular ancient sport of sumo wrestling.

Springtime in Japan may be better known for its vaunted cherry blossoms, but its annual flesh-to-flesh pounding sumo tournaments are no less thrilling. Watching these 300-pound (140 kg) humans fight is a strange experience, best viewed in its native Japan, where sumo is the Japanese NFL, albeit more than a thousand years older than football.

Springtime draws sumo fans and Japanese tourists enjoying Golden Week, a seven-day period from late April to early May containing four national holidays, including the former emperor's birthday, Greenery Day, and Children's Day.

The two, 15-day springtime sumo tournaments—in March in Osaka and May in Tokyo—are epic events that draw rowdy crowds, the antithesis to Kyoto's gentle flower-snapping set. Osaka's tournament is held at Osaka Prefectural Gymnasium (aka the Bodymaker Colosseum) and is nicknamed the "Rough Spring Tournament." It features matches between lowest to junior-grade wrestlers that are not usually televised.

Tokyo's tournaments are bigger spectacles, where grand champions are bestowed their titles. Visitors also will find the Sumo Museum there and peruse everything from woodblock prints and *banzuke* (rankings) to ceremonial aprons worn by champion wrestlers of the past.

PLANNING Sumo tournaments and the Sumo Museum www.sumo.or.jp. Japanese sumo is run by the Nihon Sumo Kyokai (Japan Sumo Association). Visitors may buy tickets online a month before the tournaments.

IN THE KNOW
Sumo: A Primer

Sumo wrestlers, called *rikishi* or *osumo-san,* lose when any part of their body (besides their feet) touches the *dohyo* (circular ring) or when they are pushed or thrown outside of it. Hair pulling, ear boxing, choking, closed-fist punching, and crotch hitting are forbidden. There are more than 60 official *kimarite* (winning techniques), but only a dozen are seen regularly. Of course, weight matters; nicknamed the "Dump Truck," Konishiki Yasokichi's peak was 630 pounds (286 kg), the heaviest on record. Wrestlers have their own official dish, *chanko nabe,* a protein-rich stew made from chicken, beef, daikon, and tofu, served with rice and beer for maximum caloric intake.

Professional sumo wrestlers, dressed in their ceremonial *kesho-mawashi,* circle around the referee during the ring-entering ceremony, the *dohyo-iri.*

Meijyo Park's cherry blossoms frame Nagoya Castle to perfection.

ASIA
JAPAN

Join in the country's cherry-blossom-viewing frenzy that kicks off the spring season.

Cherry trees are found throughout the temperate world, but only in Japan have the pink blossoms that usher in the start of spring risen to the level of a national obsession. Tokyo resident and marketing consultant Debbie Howard, a confessed "freak about cherry blossoms," describes two schools of *hanami* (flower viewing) in Japan: "walk-through" advocates who try to see as many cherry groves as possible during the peak time, and "Zen" viewers who max out their experience at one especially good spot. She prefers the latter approach: "It's very special to sit down and party under the cherry blossoms with friends."

Hanami nomads should pack a good pair of walking shoes and a map or GPS showing the best blossom-viewing spots in a given city. Those who prefer to picnic should bring a blanket to their chosen spot, plus fresh food (like sushi or sashimi) from a local market and a flask of preheated sake to take the edge off the spring chill. Howard advises viewing both in daytime and after dark, when many groves are artfully illuminated. Among her favorite hanami spots are Tokyo's Meguro River and Ueno Park, where you can float through the pink landscape on a rented boat.

PLANNING Japan www.jnto.go.jp. **Cherry Blossom Festival** For the official annual forecast for major cherry blossom destinations, go to www.jnto.go.jp/sakura; another good source is www.japan-guide.com/blog/sakura12, written by local correspondents.

BEST OF THE BEST
Floral Fortresses

The parks and gardens of Japan's great medieval castles are among the best spots for cherry blossom viewing.

● **HIMEJI CASTLE:** This sprawling medieval bastion near Kobe is almost perfectly preserved. The parkland on the north flank is flush with cherry trees. www.himeji-castle.gr.jp

● **HIROSAKI CASTLE:** Little remains of the original medieval citadel, but the castle's 120 acres (49 ha) in northern Honshu contain more than 2,600 cherry trees. www.hirosaki.co.jp

● **TAKADA CASTLE:** Surrounded by a moat, the grounds of this 17th-century castle in Joetsu on the Sea of Japan boast more than 4,000 cherry trees. The scene is especially magical at night when the blossoms are lit by thousands of lanterns. www.jnto.go.jp/eng

SUM

FIREWORK EXTRAVAGANZAS, WILD
HORSES, NEVER-ENDING SUNSHINE,
AND FESTIVALS GALORE

MER

Even in midsummer, surfers rely on wet suits to ward off the chill of England's waters.

Don't surprise the locals. Keep the conversation, or at least a "Hey bear, hey bear" mantra, going on your walk to Anan Creek's bear-viewing area.

ALASKA

Get a goose-bumps good look at some of Alaska's most famous and magnificent residents.

Biology demands it: If you want to see Alaska's bears, summer is a must. Once the season hits, both black bears and grizzlies (called brown bears on the coast) come out of hibernation, intent on mating, teaching their young essential life skills, and bulking up for their next long winter's nap. During Alaska summers, all the world becomes a bear's pantry as the waterways begin to crowd with salmon and, later, bushes hang heavy with blueberries, crowberries, and soapberries.

When it comes to wildlife viewing, there are, of course, no guarantees. But if you want a much better than average chance to see bears in their natural habitat, the state is loaded with opportunities. Hikers or strollers out wandering the in-city trails of parks right in Anchorage have even been known to get their fair share of up-close-and-personal experiences with bears.

Brenda Schwartz, a Wrangell, Alaska–based artist and bear-viewing and river guide, grew up going out to Anan Creek, a "really rich ecosystem" that's a popular fishing spot for both brown and black bears, eagles, and more. Though it's now highly regulated by the Forest Service, that hasn't dampened Schwartz's enthusiasm: "It's a great place to watch people's eyes just light up."

During Alaska summers, all the world becomes a bear's pantry as the waterways begin to crowd with salmon and, later, bushes hang heavy with blueberries, crowberries, and soapberries.

A bear cub tests out its climbing skills in its efforts to get a good look at visitors on the nearby viewing stand.

A bed of geraniums provides an ideal resting place for two bear cubs at Kodiak National Wildlife Refuge.

Keep in mind: Just because it's summer, that doesn't mean Alaska will always feel summery. Fleece and rain gear are essential Alaska equipment all summer long.

ANAN CREEK

After a boat ride from Wrangell, follow your guide down the trail to meet up with a ranger and then to the viewing platform. There's a good chance for bear sightings all along the way. After all, the Forest Service may have laid down a wooden walkway here, but they did it over existing bear trails—and the bears still use the paths. Out on the viewing platform—and in a photo blind below—you'll often find yourself surrounded by bears hungry for the fatted salmon coming up the creek. (Don't hang your toes over the edge of the platform or you could end up with a grizzly sniffing at your tootsies.) "Just watching their daily lives at that closeness is an amazing treat," Schwartz says.

KATMAI NATIONAL PARK

There's no road into Katmai. You day-trip into the park, across the Gulf of Alaska from Wrangell, by floatplane. Your pilot and guide (at times, one and the same person) will watch for bears from the air and, once spotted, set down on the water in areas with wonderful names like Geographic Harbor or Hallo Bay. Then, follow your guide's every instruction— she knows bear behavior and will keep you safe as your group tracks grizzlies, getting as close as 50 yards (46 m). For platform viewing or overnight accommodations in Katmai, book a trip to Brooks Camp (see sidebar).

KODIAK NATIONAL WILDLIFE REFUGE

While a ratio of 3,000 Kodiak brown bears to 1.9 million acres (769,000 ha) might not sound overly impressive, it is. Kodiaks like to keep a little space from their neighbors, so the wildlife refuge actually has a fairly sizable population—and each member is of incredible size. The bears can grow as large as 1,400 pounds (640 kg).

Hire a guide and head out to Frazer Lake by floatplane to see these behemoths in action. But, while there, keep your eyes open for the area's other mammals; there's a chance you'll spot some red foxes and river otters, or a tundra vole or two. Other living thrills abound. Fingers crossed, you'll get to see flocks of puffins speed on by; it's nearly impossible to keep from getting giddy when that happens.

PLANNING **Alaska** www.travelalaska.com. **Anchorage Park Foundation** www.anchorage parkfoundation.org. **Anan Creek** www.fs.usda .gov. To book a tour with Brenda Schwartz, www.alaskaupclose.com. For information about visiting Wrangell, www.wrangell.com. Learn more about Anan's bears at Wrangell's annual summer BearFest *(www.alaskabearfest .org).* **Katmai National Park** www.nps.gov/ katm. **Kodiak National Wildlife Refuge** www.fws.gov/refuge/Kodiak. For day trips into Katmai or Kodiak Refuge, consider Kodiak-based Sea Hawk Air *(www.seahawkair.com)* or Homer-based Bald Mountain Air Service *(www.baldmountainair.com).*

GREAT STAYS
Brooks Camp, Katmai National Park

There's just one campground in Katmai, **Brooks Camp,** and it's near a top bear-viewing spot. On the beach of Naknek Lake (where, hopefully, you'll get to see bears do some bathing), the campground offers a view of Dumpling Mountain along with all the necessities (though this is still bear country, so stay alert at all times). Want to skip out on cooking? Book the meal plan at nearby Brooks Lodge. (You'll have to DIY before or after the summer season.) Remember to bring a food cache (essential) and an electric fence (highly recommended). Bears may hibernate, but they don't necessarily follow the campground schedule. www.nps.gov/katm

Salmon beware—it's feeding time at Katmai National Park.

WHALE AND DOLPHIN VIEWINGS

Visit great mammals of the sea in their summer getaways.

SAGUENAY–ST. LAWRENCE MARINE PARK
Quebec, Canada

The meeting point of the St. Lawrence River and the Atlantic Ocean is a safe haven for large marine life. In addition to the world's largest mammal, the 100-foot (30 m) blue whale, the St. Lawrence estuary is home to 1,000 belugas. For a closer look, take a sea excursion by boat or kayak.

www.quebecmaritime.ca

BAY OF FUNDY
New Brunswick/Nova Scotia, Canada

The Bay of Fundy attracts the largest population of North Atlantic right whales—one of the most endangered whale species. With some of the world's highest tides, the bay amasses large quantities of zooplankton, attracting up to 12 different kinds of whales. Each summer, the Grand Manan Basin becomes the right whale's primary nursery and feeding ground.

www.bayoffundytourism.com

BAFFIN BAY–DAVIS STRAIT
Nunavut, Canada/Greenland

Every summer, the ice in the North Atlantic's Baffin Bay melts away to become a marine feeding ground, welcoming one of the longest-living animals on Earth—the bowhead whale. Reaching ages exceeding 100 years, bowheads follow a migration pattern in association with ice floes. Characterized by their large heads, bowheads are capable of breaking through sea ice at least eight inches (20 cm) thick.

www.polarcruises.com

CHANNEL ISLANDS NATIONAL PARK
California

Close to 30 species of cetaceans (whales, dolphins, and porpoises) visit Channel Islands National Park, providing numerous opportunities to encounter these majestic creatures. Hike to a lookout, scale the visitor center tower, or—for a closer look—book a boat tour.

www.nps.gov/chis/index.htm

GULF OF MAINE
New England

After a long winter in the West Indies, humpbacks and newly born calves begin their journey to New England feeding grounds in the Gulf of Maine. By May, most have arrived and can be seen near the Stellwagen Bank National Marine Sanctuary's various locations in eastern Massachusetts.

stellwagen.noaa.gov

INDIAN RIVER LAGOON
Palm Bay, Florida

North America's most diverse estuary system, the Indian River Lagoon is home to more than 2,000 species of plants and animals. The bottlenose dolphins found in the lagoon are smaller and have longer flippers than their ocean relatives. Encounter the fascinating behavior of these gentle and playful creatures on a daily Dolphin Discovery tour, guided by a certified Florida Coastal Naturalist.

www.marinediscoverycenter.org

BAJA CALIFORNIA
Mexico

Gray whales travel 12,000 miles (19,300 km) in migration—the longest of any mammal on Earth—from the freezing feeding waters of Alaska's Bering Sea to the balmy breeding grounds of Mexico's lagoons, where they provide a prime destination for whale-loving vacationers.

www.bajawhales.com

THE AZORES
Portugal

Aside from the Azores' magnificent mountain expanses and coastal scenery, this mid-Atlantic Portuguese archipelago is one of the world's best whale-watching destinations, attracting humpback, pilot, fin, minke, and blue whales. Pico Island ("the village of whales") offers an eight-day B&B package that includes several whale- and dolphin-watching boat excursions.

www.steppesdiscovery.co.uk

RURUTU
French Polynesia

Surrounded by a barrier reef, Rurutu is known for being in a prime humpback whale migration pathway and plays host to much calving, nursing, and mating. Boats depart from Moerai for trips to whale-watch, witness mothers playing with their calves, and listen to the underwater opera amplified by the coral seabed.

www.tahiti-tourism.com

DISCO BAY
Greenland

About 15 species of whales visit Greenland each year, but the narwhal—the unicorn of the sea—is among the stars. This elusive whale is known for its long, distinctive spiral tusk. At times, males can be seen surfacing the water mid-joust.

www.greenland-travel.com

A humpback whale's tail flukes disappear into the Pacific Ocean.

Sandra Bernhard

Lopez Island, Washington

Lopez Island is a wonderful spot out in the San Juan chain. The ferry trip over from Anacortes takes around an hour and a half, and on a sunny June day, you can feel all the strains falling away. I sat inside by the window watching whitecaps, but I could have stood out on the deck like my brother and his family did.

We caravanned out to MacKaye Harbor, where our friends, longtime residents of Lopez, loaned us their groovy getaway pad. Funky, simple, A-framed. We unloaded our gear and headed out for provisions. All over the island are farms that operate on the honor system; lockers filled with frozen beef and lamb, organic veggies are yours for the purchase without anyone to ring you up. Trust is big out in the San Juans.

We discovered Vortex, an organic café that serves up fresh juices, amazing salads, tostadas, and chocolate chip cookies for a pleasing lunch.

You keep moving, though. There are endless hikes, bike rides and beach exploration, wildflowers, driftwood, mosses, canopies of trees everywhere you turn taking you away into dreamscapes.

Plans came fast and furious: a brisk walk through the woods to a high bluff outlook known as Iceberg Point. "Magnificent" would not be an overstatement for the almost 360-degree views it provides. Time to sit on the rocks, staring out and clearing one's mind.

June weather can be unpredictable in the Northwest. Clouds may gather and disperse at will, but this did not deter us. We drove to Crowfoot Farm to pick organic strawberries. I kept my haul to two paper cartons' worth, but my family went a little nuts, clearing a row or two by themselves.

Without Internet connection, as the Lopezians have wisely forbidden the towers on the island, you are permitted to do all the simple things you would never entertain back home: sketching, wandering, creating a tiny wildflower bouquet to set on your daughter's pillow, or dozing off on a blanket in the high grasses of the backyard. You are off the hook.

Soon it would be back to the hustle and grind. I was already figuring out how to get back here next June.

One-woman shows keep actor, author, comedian, and musician Sandra Bernhard on the road much of the year and reunited with old friends. Nothing like the smell of jet fuel in your hair.

"Without Internet connection ... you are permitted to do all the simple things you would never entertain back home: sketching, wandering, creating a tiny wildflower bouquet to set on your daughter's pillow."

Sunset at Lopez Island's Shark Reef Sanctuary offers a typical island respite from mainland life.

CALIFORNIA/OREGON/WASHINGTON

PACIFIC CREST TRAIL

"Mile for mile, I can't think of another long-distance trail that rivals the Pacific Crest Trail. The trail is rarely crowded and almost always perfectly graded; in summer, the weather is consistently sunny, dry, and warm; and the scenery is world-class, highlighted by two of my most favorite locales, the High Sierra and North Cascades."

—ANDREW SKURKA, AUTHOR OF NATIONAL GEOGRAPHIC'S
THE ULTIMATE HIKER'S GEAR GUIDE

One of America's National Scenic Trails, the Pacific Crest Trail makes its way from Mexico to Canada, spanning 2,650 miles (4,265 km). The popular hiking and equestrian route snakes through California, Oregon, and Washington. *Pictured:* Upper Sardine Lake in California's Tahoe National Forest

TELLURIDE

Pick your pleasure when the canyon town becomes a summer playground of festivals and fun for big kids.

Hit Telluride on a high summer day, and it's like landing in North America's Shangri-La: a perfect, protected box canyon, so narrow it almost seems as if you can reach out and touch both sides. At the end of the canyon overlooking Telluride, the 365-foot (111 m) Bridal Veil Falls looks like a prop for postcard photographers. The air smells of forest and altitude, like skiers whose clothes have dried after yet another epic winter.

On the streets of Telluride, which look about the same as they did in the mining heyday of the Old West, plan tomorrow by playing Telluride profiler, when you pick your hangout by the people on the open-air patios: Mountain bikers have bigger shoulders, mountain climbers bigger calves, rock climbers bigger mugs of beer, fishermen the biggest lies, and white-water rafters are still shaking river out of their ears. The spagoers are the relaxed ones, sipping an aperitif glass of wine.

No point in hurrying. Summer lasts until the closing credits of Labor Day's Telluride Film Festival. The altitude in this corner of southwest Colorado takes some getting used to, anyway. Maybe that's what's causing the heavy breathing. Or maybe it's just the sound of another group of mountain bikers coming in for the night.

PLANNING Telluride www.telluride.com. **Telluride Film Festival** www.telluridefilmfestival.org. For the film festival, advance planning for tickets and a place to stay are vital.

BEST OF THE BEST
Telluride's Summer Festivals

Telluride in the summer hosts film, wine, and balloon festivals, but box-canyon acoustics mean bonus points for the biggest party, June's Telluride Bluegrass Festival. Name acts from around the world come to play; mandolins and banjos become as common as looking for a parking place. Sometimes, the very best music is at the campsites; jam sessions spring up like mushrooms watered by the mist coming off the waterfall at the valley's head. It doesn't matter if you don't know your Flatt from your Scruggs: Toes will be tapping. www.bluegrass.com/telluride

The lineup at the annual Telluride Film Festival gives fair competition to a hike in the surrounding mountains.

Though the area is famous for its tart cherries, Traverse City—and its National Cherry Festival—also welcomes fans of the fruit's sweet varieties.

MICHIGAN

TRAVERSE CITY

Bliss out on an endless array of cherry concoctions in the epicenter of cherry country.

To enter the northwest corner of Michigan's Lower Peninsula in July is to land in cherry heaven: The region produces more than half of the U.S. tart cherry crop, not to mention plenty of the sweet kind, too. Traverse City celebrates the fruit with its National Cherry Festival, held in venues throughout the city.

"You're greeted with fresh cherries right when you arrive," says festival marketing manager Susan Wilcox Olson. Freshly picked ones.

Then plunge into cherry overdrive. Kids can do it face-first (read on). A slice of the event's signature pie, cherry crumb, is a must. Wash it down with a cold glass of cherry lemonade in the park at the foot of Grand Traverse Bay. Stock up on preserves and sample cherry barbecue, jerky, and mustard at the waterfront farmers' market. Assuage your guilt in a footrace along the coastlines of the East and West Bays. The runners' reward: a fresh cup of cherries as they cross the finish line.

And what would a cherry festival be without a cherry pie-eating contest? The ones here are for youngsters. "They're no-hands, face down into a slice of pie," Wilcox Olson says. "At the end, you've got all these kids with huge, happy red smiles."

PLANNING National Cherry Festival www.cherryfestival.org.

BEST OF THE BEST
The Old Mission Peninsula

The Old Mission Peninsula extends 22 miles (35 km) into Grand Traverse Bay, separating its east and west arms. Studded with wineries, orchards, antique shops, and cozy inns, the narrow stretch offers stunning views of rolling vineyards descending to azure waters on both sides. Take a leisurely road trip, pausing to snack on cherries and apples at roadside stands and farm markets. Stop in for ice cream or picnic supplies at the Old Mission General Store, which dates from the mid-1800s, then head for the water at Haserot Beach, tucked into a harbor near the tip of the peninsula. www.oldmission.com

SHOWSTOPPING OUTDOOR MUSIC VENUES

Listen, watch, and marvel at open-air stages as great as the performances on them.

GREAT STAGE PARK

Manchester, Tennessee

If you're after a really good time, then it's off to Bonnaroo, a music festival that takes over the 700-acre (285 ha) Great Stage Park every June. It is a giant party, though you'll need to get ready for crowds and the Southern sun. Maybe some mud, too. But it's all worth it: The lineup, from jam bands and rock royalty to bluegrass and funk, is a music lover's dream.
www.bonnaroo.com

RED ROCKS PARK AND AMPHITHEATRE

Denver, Colorado

This one is nature made—big-time. The only acoustically perfect, naturally occurring amphitheater in the world, the well-named Red Rocks serves up the kind of audio experience engineers work a lifetime to perfect. And the visuals? Two brilliant red sandstone monoliths rise 300 feet (90 m) above the crowd.
www.redrocksonline.com

THE GREEK THEATRE

Los Angeles, California

You'll go for the main act, but, thanks to the Griffith Park location and the stellar sound system, you'll remember the Greek. With just 5,800 seats, you'll never feel like you're out at sea (or, more importantly, can't see) at the Greek; it's one of the most intimate outdoor venues you'll ever experience.
www.greektheatrela.com

DOWNTOWN MONTREAL

Montreal, Quebec, Canada

For ten days every summer, a wide swath of downtown Montreal turns into one of the ultimate city music venues. All traffic comes to a halt once the annual Festival International de Jazz de Montréal kicks off. Then it's just people and music, from the namesake jazz to blues to rock.
www.montrealjazzfest.com

SLANE CASTLE

Meath, Ireland

It takes a mighty backdrop to (just about) overshadow outsized performers like Madonna, U2, and the Rolling Stones. But if any venue can do it, it's Slane Castle, the current residence of Lord Henry Montcharles, Eighth Marquess Conyngham, whose family has called Slane home since 1701. The estate's natural amphitheater below the castle is worthy of rock royalty. With a history that includes King George VI and St. Patrick himself, Slane Castle is legendary—and so are its shows.
www.slanecastle.ie

DALHALLA AMPHITHEATER

Near Rättvik, Sweden

There are few outdoor concert spots cooler (literally or figuratively) than an old limestone quarry. The terraced gray stone and pool of aqua water at the bottom create an arresting backdrop and add up to a striking photo op. Make your day at Dalhalla a double bill: Take one of the guided tours before the night's event begins.

AUDITORIUM PARCO DELLA MUSICA

Rome, Italy

This modern, Renzo Piano–designed music complex actually recalls the theaters of ancient Rome. The 3,000-seat open-air space is, very much, of its city—and the acoustics aren't bad, either.
www.auditorium.com

FLOATING OPERA STAGE OF THE BREGENZ FESTIVAL

Vienna, Austria

This is an opera stage on a lake. Every year since 1946, the Bregenz Festival creates amazing floating stages with sets as much a treat for the eyes as the music is for the ears.
www.bregenzerfestspiele.com

SULTAN'S POOL

Jerusalem, Israel

The Ottoman sultan Suleiman the Magnificent brought this ancient pool of water back to life in the 16th century. Five hundred years later, during summers when it is dry, the area is put to use to refresh people in a different way: with music.
www.gojerusalem.com/discover/item_30/Sultans-Pool

ETHNOMIR

Near Moscow, Russia

Every summer since 2008, this cultural complex hosts the Dikaya Myata (Wild Mint Music Festival) to become the Russian version of Max Yasgur's Woodstock farm. The open-air, multiday music festival, about a half hour outside Moscow, features musicians from Russia, Germany, the U.S., and elsewhere.
eng.mintmusic.ru

The floating stages built for Austria's annual Bregenz Festival heighten the drama of every opera performance. Here, a rehearsal of Umberto Giordano's *Andrea Chénier.*

Visitors get a sky-high, 360-degree view of the Iowa State Fair during a spin on one of the fairground's many colorful amusement rides.

IOWA

DES MOINES

Join the Iowa State Fair's classic American celebration of agriculture and community—and eat all your meals on a stick.

As August's sultry summer days herald the home stretch of the growing season, rural and urban Iowans gather for a ten-day party to celebrate the state's rich farming heritage and to challenge visitors—and each other—to a bit of friendly, down-home competition. Held in historic Des Moines barns that have housed fairgoing livestock for more than a century, the Iowa State Fair attracts the biggest cows, the heftiest pigs, and the most successful harvests—all integral to a state whose engine is driven by agriculture. The spirit of healthy competition reaches beyond farming, too. Challenge yourself to a ride on the notorious double Ferris wheel, check out the world-famous butter cow, or take on the task of eating three meals a day—from breakfast eggs to pork chops—on a stick.

Livestock and produce contests, however, are the fair's lifeblood. Judging is done the old-fashioned way, with blue ribbons coveted by the best cattle breeders and tomato growers alike. "I love the animal judging," says historian Thomas Leslie. "When you watch sheep being judged, you start to learn why things like muscular balance are important to farmers and the rest of the state. We're all here because of the farmers."

PLANNING Iowa State Fair www.iowastatefair.org. Flights arrive into Des Moines International Airport from around the country. Fair tickets can be purchased in advance online.

IN THE KNOW
Win a Blue Ribbon

For those of us who may not have a best-in-class pig or a 3.5-pound (1.6 kg) tomato, there are plenty of other chances for Joe or Jane Fairgoer to make the cut. Each year, special events like chess tournaments, fiddling contests, spelling bees, and yo-yo competitions make it possible for anyone to participate and take home a prize. Sign-ups typically take place 30 to 60 minutes in advance. "There are competitions for everything," historian Thomas Leslie says. "It's about having fun and being a good sport." All part and parcel of the Iowa character. www.iowastate fair.org/competition/categories

QUEBEC, CANADA

MONTREAL

Surround yourself with silliness when this cultured capital turns itself inside out—and backwards—for July's Just for Laughs comedy extravaganza.

Come July, Montreal removes all vestiges of its frosty mantle and gets its funny on—seriously. Absurdity fills the cosmopolitan streets around the Quartier des Spectacles, Montreal's cultural hub bounded by theaters, restaurants, and museums.

The Just for Laughs festival provokes bilingual chuckles throughout the month, when countless comedians and quirky acts in French and English take over the city. And where would the fun be if it were all hidden inside the city's many theaters and clubs? Much of the real craziness occurs *en plein air*. Explains festival president Andy Nulman: "We close off downtown and make it our playground. We've had big foam parties with thousands of pounds of soap suds."

In the swirl of the crowd, dodge can-can dancers on stilts and Les Grosses Têtes ("the Big Heads"), human caricatures with enormous noggins. Brace yourself for a ribbing from the smart-aleck Mauvaises Langues, street performers dressed as tongues who will give you a verbal lashing in French. And watch out for the occasional runaway bus. "We once wrapped a city bus to make it look like it was driving backwards," Nulman recalls. "Being a comedy festival, we can get away with things that would get other people arrested."

PLANNING Montreal Just for Laughs Festival www.hahaha.com. For major savings on show tickets, pick up a passport on the site under "Special Offers."

FOR FOODIES
Eating on the Go

Grab a quick bite between laughs at the Food Souk, the festival's bustling roundup of Montreal's most popular food trucks and stands in the Quartier des Spectacles. The souk is open every day of the festival on Rue Sainte-Catherine; adventurous eaters can sample diverse options from upscale *poutine* (a gloppy concoction of fries, cheese, and gravy) made with foie gras to Japanese *takoyaki* to frozen treats. Crunch into a pork *banh mi* taco from Grumman '78, which launched the Food Souk, or sink your teeth into the aptly named Le Decadent, a gooey explosion of salty and sweet from La Mangeoire: a grilled peanut butter, Nutella, and bacon sandwich. www.grumman78.com

All the world's a comedy stage—sidewalks and streets included—when the annual Just for Laughs Festival takes over downtown Montreal.

Christopher Buckley

Meteors Over Maine

Every early August, when my now-grown children were still growing and at an age when looking up at the night sky was more wondrous than looking down at the screen of an iPhone, we would start to count down the days until the start of the annual Perseid meteor shower. Thinking back on their genuine excitement over it makes me—now an old man of 60—a bit watery about the eyes.

We spent those summers in Maine, in a magical little coastal town called Blue Hill. The cabin that we rented was on a magical cove with the somewhat less magical name of Stinky Cove. I emphasize that it was no longer stinky by the time our era arrived.

Our view was to the north—ideal for meteor-shower viewing. And if we were lucky, there would *not* be a full moon to cast occluding light. In early August, no moon was best of all.

So just after dusk, we'd sit on the deck and tilt our chairs back so as not to get cricks in our necks and . . . watch. I would offer a reward for whoever saw the first one. When the kids were very young, a quarter would suffice, but as they got older and more mercenary, a dollar became the going rate.

And then one of them would cry out, "There!" And suddenly *there* would be a fiery little streak in the sky. Then another. And another. On a really good Perseid shower night, we'd might count, oh, 30 or more, depending on how long the kids were willing to postpone going back inside to watch *The Little Mermaid* or *The Adventures of Milo and Otis*.

You can see this amazing annual spectacle all over the Northern Hemisphere. But for us, there was no better observatory than the wooden deck and the still waters of Stinky Cove. If the water was really still that night, which in my memory it always is, you could actually see the reflection of the meteors on the mirror-surface of the cove, to the sound of loon call. Sometimes, added to that haunting, mournful sound track might come the raucous belching of seals, sated on a school of herring—a ridiculous, loud sound that always made us giggle.

Christopher Buckley is the author of 15 books, most recently the novel They Eat Puppies, Don't They?

"*My now-grown children were still growing and at an age when looking up at the night sky was more wondrous than looking down at the screen of an iPhone.*"

Maine's night sky offers plenty of visual company as you watch for the Perseid meteor shower's speedy streakers.

RHODE ISLAND

NEWPORT

Hear legends and discover new sounds at the Newport Folk and Jazz festivals, living embodiments of America's musical history.

In late July and early August, the population of Newport swells and the panorama of aristocratic white yachts seemingly painted into Narragansett Bay becomes the backdrop for a stage. Part of Newport's summertime resort tradition since 1954, the Jazz Festival has sprouted a six-decade legacy, bred the equally iconic Newport Folk Festival, and inspired an era of music festivals from Woodstock to Lollapalooza. "Name a legend—Bob Dylan, Joan Baez, Johnny Cash," challenges Folk Festival producer Jay Sweet. "They've all played Newport." The same goes for the Jazz Festival, where all-stars like Duke Ellington jump-started their careers.

International reputations dwarf the festivals' humble setting—a historic fort that maxes out at around 10,000 attendees. Fully concentrated days mean constantly hopping between tents. The Folk Festival's distinct iPod-shuffle feel, where bluegrass is juxtaposed alongside indie rock, broadens your ear and the boundaries of musical genres.

Beyond music, fans come for the sense of congregation that characterizes the lollipop of land sticking out into the harbor. "Singing 'This Land Is Your Land' along with 93-year-old Pete Seeger while all these people around you are bawling their eyes out," says Sweet, "makes you feel part of something way bigger than yourself."

PLANNING Newport Jazz Festival newportjazzfest.net. **Newport Folk Festival** www.newportfolkfest .net Tickets can be purchased online. The Newport County Convention and Visitors Bureau *(www.gonewport .com)* offers information about getting to Newport and accommodations.

It takes a stellar lineup to steal attention away from Newport's waterfront, but festivalgoers only have eyes (and ears) for the musicians.

BEST OF THE BEST
Newport Cliff Walk

Sandwiched between the rugged, rocky Atlantic coastline and the backyards of mansions reminiscent of European aristocracy, the Newport Cliff Walk is a 3.5-mile (5.6 km) trail with stunning views. Largely built in the late 19th and early 20th centuries, Newport's mansions were summer "cottages" for some of America's wealthiest families whose investments during the industrial revolution paid off. Meandering over private property, the trail is protected as a sphere of public domain thanks to colonial-era edicts. Some of the historic mansions along the way are open to the public as museums, including the Breakers and Marble House, both of which belonged to the Vanderbilt family. www.newportmansions.org

Flags, back-in-time costumes, and plenty of smiles pave the way for a not-politics-as-usual feel during Washington, D.C.'s Fourth of July celebrations.

UNITED STATES

WASHINGTON, D.C.

Immerse yourself in the capital's celebrations of independence—and other cultures—for the Fourth of July.

Not too surprisingly, the nation's capital puts on a really big show for the Fourth of July. And the thousands who gather there know it. The sense of community is palpable in spite of—or maybe because of—the crush of people sweating together on the National Mall's grassy expanse under the iconic dome of the U.S. Capitol as the sticky summer sun sets. "People from all over the world were gathered," marvels Pavel Romanenko, a Russian-born expatriate who says the celebration made him feel "part of American history."

In the afternoon, top musicians, accompanied by the National Symphony Orchestra, put on a free concert. Then, after the sun sets, the crowd's attention turns to the pointy tip of the Washington Monument as fireworks create an explosive dialogue in the sky above it.

Another nice bonus of the July spectacle is the Smithsonian Folklife Festival, also on the Mall. The ten-day event features music concerts, dance programs, and hands-on workshops showcasing worldwide cultural traditions—in recent years, the festival has featured everything from folk music in Central Asia and storytelling in Appalachia to body and street art in New York City. You'll find the two outdoor celebrations are a natural fit. As Smithsonian curator Betty Belanus notes, "Programs about independence traditions from around the world relate to the festival's goal of celebrating and humanizing diversity."

PLANNING Washington, D.C. washington.org. **Smithsonian Folklife Festival** www.festival.si.edu.

IN THE KNOW
Nearby Fireworks

Find impressive fireworks and more a short drive from the throngs at the National Mall.

● **FREDERICK, MARYLAND:** Walk Frederick's colonial-era streets before gathering in Baker Park for the annual fireworks display. www.celebratefrederick.com

● **LEESBURG, VIRGINIA:** Celebrate where the Declaration of Independence and Constitution were hidden from the British during the War of 1812 with a downtown parade and fireworks show in Ida Lee Park. www.idalee.org

● **MOUNT VERNON, VIRGINIA:** Daytime smoke fireworks add color to the afternoon sky over the Potomac River by George Washington's home. www.mountvernon.org

LOCAL FOURTH
OF JULY CELEBRATIONS

Feel the Independence Day spirit at these quintessential American festivities.

INDEPENDENCE, CALIFORNIA

Venture to the remote eastern Sierra east of Kings Canyon National Park to celebrate the small town of Independence's favorite day. Watch fireworks glow against the snowcapped mountain backdrop, chow down on pancakes and homemade pie in the park, and join the floats and fire engines in the community parade.

www.independence-ca.com

TELLURIDE, COLORADO

Save room at the Volunteer Fire Department's July 4 barbecue for the free root beer floats on tap at the Telluride Mining Museum. Located in southwestern Colorado's San Juan Mountains, this historic gold-rush town turned world-class ski resort goes all out for Independence Day with F-16 flyovers, fireworks, and a quirky Main Street parade.

www.visittelluride.com

BISBEE, ARIZONA

The longest and fastest running Fourth of July tradition in this former Old West copper mining camp is a 1.5-mile (2.4 km) coaster-car race down Tombstone Canyon Road. Cheer on the young drivers (ages 9–16), then, after the town's parade, head over to Brewery Gulch to watch traditional mining contests like mucking (shoveling broken rock into a bucket) and hard rock drilling.

www.discoverbisbee.com

SEGUIN, TEXAS

Follow the flag-waving crowds 40 minutes northeast of San Antonio to downtown Seguin, home to the "Biggest Small Town Fourth of July Parade in Texas." This multiday celebration includes a food-and-music Freedom Fiesta and a Fiesta Swim at the Wave Pool.

www.seguintexas.gov

SEWARD, NEBRASKA

Named "America's Fourth of July city–small town USA" by congressional proclamation, this former prairie settlement city about 30 minutes west of Lincoln has hosted a star-spangled Independence Day celebration since 1868. Student and civic groups coordinate the day's events, ranging from a grand parade and Wild West shoot-out to apple-pie-eating contests and clogging.

www.julyfourthseward.com

HANNIBAL, MISSOURI

National Tom Sawyer Days add a Mark Twain twist to the Fourth of July in Missouri's beloved river town. The multi-day event (typically four days, including July 4) features the National Fence Painting Contest, live music, mud volleyball, and a competitive frog jump for little kids and their favorite amphibians.

www.visithannibal.com

MACKINAC ISLAND, MICHIGAN

Hire a horse-drawn taxi to clip-clop between Independence Day activities on car-free Mackinac. The island's simply patriotic July 4 pastimes typically include old-fashioned three-legged races, an egg toss, and the All-American Picnic at Revolutionary-era Fort Mackinac. At dusk, spread a blanket at the shore to watch the fireworks.

www.mackinacisland.org

CLINTON, TENNESSEE

Step inside the Museum of Appalachia's split-rail fences to experience the pioneer-era July 4 Celebration and Anvil Shoot. There's bluegrass music, bell ringing, rail-splitting, and dulcimermaking, but the highlight is seeing (and hearing) 100-pound (45 kg) iron anvils jettisoned into the air by exploding gunpowder. The living history village-farm is 16 miles (28 km) north of Knoxville.

museumofappalachia.org

MURRELLS INLET, SOUTH CAROLINA

In the laid-back "seafood capital of South Carolina," the Fourth of July parade is quintessentially low-country. At high tide, a flotilla of decorated fishing, shrimp, and pleasure boats—horns blaring and flags flying—floats down the Murrells Inlet shoreline. Stroll the Marsh Walk to see the procession and the fireworks that follow.

www.murrellsinletsc.com

BAR HARBOR, MAINE

This historic resort gateway to Acadia National Park rolls out the red, white, and blue bunting for a sunrise-to-starlight community celebration. Festivities begin with an outdoor blueberry pancake breakfast and end with evening fireworks over Frenchman's Bay. In between, there's a town parade, a seafood festival, concerts, and lobster races.

www.barharborinfo.com

America's small-town celebrations—like Hannibal, Missouri's Tom Sawyer Days—practically demand that every man, woman, and child get in on the fun. Costumes are optional (but recommended).

CHINCOTEAGUE PONY SWIM

"It's one of those sights that stays with you—a flock of ponies veering into the sea, suddenly waterborne. You can't really tell if they can see the distant shore, but they're paddling like fury in that direction, so you've gotta believe they'll make it just fine. And they always do, tugging onto the sand as if they were pulling the chariot of Poseidon behind them."

—K. M. KOSTYAL, NATIONAL GEOGRAPHIC AUTHOR

During the Chincoteague Pony Swim, wild horses make their way across Virginia's Assateague Channel. This event occurs on the last Wednesday of July when the tide is calm enough to allow even the youngest ponies to make the trip safely. *Pictured:* Chincoteague horses race through the Assateague marshes.

SACSAYHUAMÁN, PERU

INTI RAYMI FESTIVAL

"The festivities culminated at the Sacsayhuamán ruins above town with Inti Raymi, a massive and tightly choreographed reenactment of the Inca Empire's most sacred rituals. Among the ancient rocks, modern-day Inca took on their ancestors' roles as kings, courtiers, provincial chiefs, and warriors, all of whom would travel from the far reaches of the empire to call Inti, the Inca sun god, back to the southern skies."

—TOM CLYNES, *NATIONAL GEOGRAPHIC ADVENTURE* MAGAZINE, NOVEMBER 2007

The celebration of Inti Raymi, the Festival of the Sun, is held annually on the Southern Hemisphere's winter solstice—the shortest day of the year. The festivities include dancing and other rituals to mark the beginning of the new year.

SUMMER SUNSETS

Let Nature's greatest light show cap the perfect end to a warm summer day.

HALEKULANI RESORT

Honolulu, Hawaii

It's a Hawaiian classic. Take a seat on the veranda. Let the breeze coming off the water, a mai tai (a house specialty), and the music start to convince you that, somehow, you should live here. Forever. The sunset—which will likely match your drink—will finish the job.

www.halekulani.com

ANTELOPE ISLAND STATE PARK

Syracuse, Utah

Sunset blooms big around the Great Salt Lake's largest island. Whether you're standing near the causeway or pulling out your camera to catch the sunset behind the island's namesake herd, you'll feel surrounded by the evening's big event.

stateparks.utah.gov/parks/antelope-island

NEW YORK HARBOR

New York, New York

Lady Liberty looks just that much more elegant with the sunset at her back. Take it all in from the deck of a classic tall ship, the sails raised high and a glass of Champagne in your hand. The views east dazzle as well, as the sun's fading light reflects softly off the glass and steel skyscrapers of Lower Manhattan.

www.manhattanbysail.com/sails

KEY WEST

Florida

No town puts on a better sunset-related shindig than Key West. Every night, starting about two hours before the disappearing sun paints the sky, head to the waterfront for some shopping and food cart delights. Then, turn toward the Gulf of Mexico and watch the natural artwork break out.

www.sunsetcelebration.org

TORRES DEL PAINE NATIONAL PARK

Chile

The park's geographic range offers a million different sunsets. But, one mental snapshot: Imagine the park's granite peaks and the glacial lakes below glowing pink. All around, spots of green moss send the blushing landscape into overdrive.

www.torresdelpaine.com/ingles

OIA CASTLE

Santorini, Greece

It's just a giant postcard. As the sun starts to slip below into the Aegean Sea, the sky all around the traditional village and castle of Oia, on the very northern tip of the island of Santorini, gives itself over from the day's magnificent blue to crimson to . . . every sunset color imaginable. Beware: It's a popular spot. But once that color starts to break out, you won't notice. It is breathtaking.

www.greeka.com/cyclades/santorini/index.htm

CLIFTON BEACHES

Cape Town, South Africa

White sand. Aqua water. Brilliant sunset sky. There's a reason Clifton is home to some of Cape Town's wealthiest residents: that view. But a shuttle ride to the area—parking is dreadful—makes it easy to take in without the house payment. Head straight to one of Clifton's four beaches. Take up temporary residence on a blanket and watch Nature's fireworks explode over the South Atlantic Ocean.

www.capetown.travel

KENTING NATIONAL PARK

Hengchun Peninsula, Taiwan

High above Kenting's western shore, this viewpoint on Taiwan's southern tip looking out over the Taiwan Strait is, surprisingly, not one of the park's most popular sights. For you, this is a good thing; you may end up with the sunset all to yourself. Keep an eye out for some of the park's other natural beauties: thousands of varieties of tropical plants, birds, and butterflies.

www.ktnp.gov.tw/eng

VAIROU BAY

Bora Bora, Tahiti

Park yourself on a deck at your resort. And just wait. As the sun meets the horizon, the world glows brilliant. Though the area's hotels are all high-end—there's a price to pay when you head to the quintessential tropical island paradise—the free evening show may be the best amenity of them all.

www.tahiti-tourisme.com

ULURU (AYERS ROCK)

Northern Territory, Australia

As the sun dips and the sky swirls through its color show, the sandstone of Uluru, a massive monolith rising 1,150 feet (350 m) from the plains of the Australian outback, glows red—nearly stealing the sky's thunder. Before choosing a spot to watch the view, consider taking a hike around the sacred site. It's farther than it looks—the rock is nearly 6 miles (10 km) in circumference.

whc.unesco.org/en/list/447

Bora Bora's postcard-perfect good looks get bumped up a notch (or 30) during every evening's sunset. Even the water seems to soak up the color.

The only thing to expect at the Fringe Festival: the unexpected. Here, the Kataklo dance theater group gets their bikes in on the act.

SCOTLAND

EDINBURGH

The capital city discards its dreary coat for a summer filled with music, comedy, dancing, and golf.

I t's a sunny summer afternoon in Edinburgh and thousands of people are roaming the streets of the Scottish capital. Some are strolling the revitalized waterfront, others are bouncing from circus show to comedy act at the city's famous summer Fringe Festival, while still others clamber over the stout walls of Edinburgh Castle—perched atop an ancient volcano. About an hour down the coast, golf pilgrims tee off at grassy seaside links where the game was born hundreds of years ago.

ENJOY THE SHOWS: FROM THE WACKY TO THE RIDICULOUS

Edinburgh's action reaches fever pitch over the last month of summer. In August, the world's single largest arts festival—the Edinburgh Fringe—takes the stage in hundreds of venues large and small all over the city. Offbeat and obscure comedy, music, dance, and drama are the forte of this wacky parallel to the highbrow Edinburgh International Festival, which takes place at the same time. The scale of the Fringe is enormous: nearly 2,700 shows at more than 250 venues attended by around two million people each year. The program alone is nearly 400 pages long, featuring acts from around the world. Many of the shows are free, all of them unusual, and some so far out they seem to come from another planet.

In August, the world's single largest arts festival—the Edinburgh Fringe—takes the stage in hundreds of venues large and small all over the city.

A bonus summer festival: More than 200,000 attend Edinburgh's Military Tattoo (an international show of military bands, color, pageantry, and theater) during its three-week run at Edinburgh Castle every year.

St. Andrews is the town that, in many ways, gave birth to today's Scotland. It's where both modern-day golf and Scotland's universities got their start.

Start with the Royal Mile. It's chockablock with buskers—fire-eaters, mimes, escape artists—strutting their stuff on the cobblestones. But it's the eclectic stage acts that bring people back to the Fringe year after year. You'll find break-dancers competing for the Scottish championship in a club near the old North Bridge, while acrobats dive into a circus-style adaptation of Dante's *Inferno* near the city's celebrated castle. Just try keeping a straight face at a musical-comedy version of the Spanish Armada at a small theater or at the somber reinterpretation of *Grease* at another.

The best way to approach the megafestivities? It's up to you. Buy tickets in advance or, suggests American musician and Fringe aficionado Matthew Peterson, just "walk around without a plan and experience all sorts of things."

WANDER THE WATERFRONT

Edinburgh's waterfront also comes alive in summer. The once hardworking port has transformed itself into a historical and cultural hub. Scramble aboard the royal yacht *Britannia* to see how the "other half" once lived. The 412-foot (126 m) steamship was the Queen's floating palace until 1997 and is now a museum (recalling its own regal history) permanently docked in Edinburgh. Then, drink in a little cultural enrichment: Learn the difference between Highland and island Scotch while lounging on a leather sofa in the wood-paneled vaults at the Scotch Malt Whisky Society.

CATCH A ROUND ON LEGENDARY GREENS

Escape the madding crowds at one of Scotland's legendary golf courses, like the storied Royal and Ancient Golf Club in St. Andrews, about 56 miles (90 km) up the east coast from Edinburgh. Founded in 1754, the club is generally regarded as the governing authority of global golf. There, you can realize the fantasy of many a golfer and play in the footsteps of Bobby Jones, Ben Hogan, Arnold Palmer, Jack Nicklaus, and Tiger Woods on the scenic Old Course, one of seven public links in the seaside city, where 12th-century shepherds knocking stones into rabbit holes with crooks and canes allegedly invented the game.

At first glance, the links look deceptively easy. But don't be lulled into a false sense of bravado: The greens are huge and notoriously tricky, more than 100 bunkers are waiting to swallow your ball, and over the back nine you'll need to conquer legendary Old Course features like Hell and the Valley of Sin.

Before you drive back to the capital, pop into the British Golf Museum with its 17,000 artifacts, including early clubs and the original 18th-century handwritten rules of golf.

PLANNING **Edinburgh** www.visitscotland.com, www.edinburgh.org. **Edinburgh Fringe Festival** www.edfringe.com. The website gives a complete rundown of the acts, the venues, and how to buy tickets. Festivalgoers often purchase tickets months in advance. **Waterfront** Royal yacht *Britannia,* www.royalyachtbritannia.co.uk; Scotch Malt Whisky Society, www.smws.co.uk. **St. Andrews** Royal and Ancient Golf Club, www.randa.org; Old Course, www.standrews.org.uk. **British Golf Museum** www.britishgolfmuseum.co.uk.

FOR FOODIES
Scottish Food in Edinburgh

When you're out and about, these restaurants are excellent, convenient eating options near Edinburgh Castle:

• **ELEPHANT HOUSE:** Haggis (the national dish), neeps (turnips), and tatties (mashed potatoes) are among the favorites at this café on George IV Bridge. J. K. Rowling is among its celebrated habitués. www.elephanthouse.biz

• **GRAIN STORE:** A cozy, medieval granary known for its nouvelle Scottish cuisine. Among the standouts: Orkney scallops ceviche and Aberdeen Angus steak with ox tongue. www.grainstore-restaurant.co.uk

• **NUMBER ONE:** With a Michelin star, this upscale restaurant in the Balmoral Hotel is one of Scotland's finest. The menu ranges from simple seafood to venison with blackberries. restaurantnumberone.com

Tao samurai drummers leap into action at a recent Fringe Festival.

SUMMER THEATER

Catch the season's best shows, from musical premieres to world-class Shakespeare productions.

STRATFORD FESTIVAL
Stratford, Ontario, Canada

The largest classical repertory theater in North America stages productions on a thrust stage where the finest Shakespearean actors perform the bard's great comedies and tragedies. Open May to September.

www.stratfordfestival.ca

NEW YORK MUSICAL THEATRE FESTIVAL
New York, New York

Each July, dozens of original musicals premiere at this festival, held in the heart of New York City's theater district. Many of the event's new musicals go on to successful Broadway or off-Broadway runs, including the Tony Award–winning *Next to Normal.*

www.nymf.org/index.html

FESTIVAL INTERNACIONAL DE TEATRO
Caracas, Venezuela

For more than 30 years, the premier theater festival in Latin America has brought together scores of performance companies from around the world to act in Venezuela's capital. Performers take to the streets, plazas, and theater venues throughout the city for two weeks each April to stage classics such as Anton Chekhov's *The Cherry Orchard,* Henrik Ibsen's *Hedda Gabler,* and Dante's *Inferno.*

fitcaracas.blogspot.com (use your translator)

EDINBURGH INTERNATIONAL FESTIVAL
Edinburgh, Scotland

Founded soon after the end of World War II, Edinburgh's annual August fest ranks as one of the leading arts celebrations in the world. Theater productions range from *Electra* to a modern-day retelling of *Macbeth.* Visit the festival headquarters in the Hub, an iconic city landmark whose spire dominates the Royal Mile between Edinburgh Castle and Holyrood Palace.

www.eif.co.uk

OPEN AIR THEATRE
Regent's Park, London, England

Vivien Leigh and Judi Dench both trod the boards of this London landmark, the oldest permanent outdoor theater in Britain. More than 130,000 spectators attend each season's four productions between May and September. Bring a hamper and sip Pimm's on the picnic lawn while enjoying the theater's signature piece, *A Midsummer Night's Dream.*

openairtheatre.org

FESTIVAL D'AVIGNON
Avignon, France

At least one new show opens every night at this festival in the south of France. Every July, Avignon becomes a "city-theater," with 20-odd historical venues transformed into performance spaces. The heart is the Cour d'Honneur, the main courtyard of the Pope's Palace, where spectators gather for performances during the Provençal summer nights.

www.festival-avignon.com/en

ZÜRCHER THEATER SPEKTAKEL
Zurich, Switzerland

Dozens of independent theater companies put on cutting-edge productions each August in one of Europe's most important contemporary performing arts festivals. Performances take place in the parklike Landiwiese on Lake Zurich, where venues include an open-air stage and a shipyard for creative staging possibilities.

www.theaterspektakel.ch

NATIONAL ARTS FESTIVAL
Grahamstown, South Africa

Bundle up for performances at Africa's largest cultural event, held in June and July in South Africa's Eastern Cape region. The children's arts festival offers drama workshops for kids ages 4–13, while street theater productions carry the festival spirit throughout the city.

www.nationalartsfestival.co.za

IIDA PUPPET FESTA
Nagano Prefecture, Japan

Known as the "city of puppet shows," Iida, located between Tokyo and Nagoya, hosts the largest puppetry festival in Japan every August. Some 150 troupes perform shows ranging from traditional Bunraku puppetry to modern acts in dozens of sites throughout the city, from Puppetry Hall to the grounds of parks and shrines.

www.city.iida.lg.jp/puppet

PERTH INTERNATIONAL ARTS FESTIVAL
Perth, Australia

Each year, Perth celebrates the oldest annual, international, multi-arts festival in the Southern Hemisphere. Founded in 1953, the three-week-long celebration includes the National Play Festival, which showcases new plays written and performed by Australia's finest theater artists. Venues include His Majesty's Theatre, the only working Edwardian theater in Australia.

www.perthfestival.com.au

During the esteemed Festival d'Avignon, the Cour d'Honneur at the Place du Palais des Papes hosts an actor with Charlie Chaplin on the brain.

NORWAY
SVALBARD

"Through binoculars he stared over the pack ice off Svalbard, that rugged Arctic archipelago between Norway and the North Pole. These bleak islands, the largest of which is Spitsbergen, are one of the strongholds of a magnificent animal we Norwegians call *isbjørn*—ice bear."

—THOR LARSEN, *NATIONAL GEOGRAPHIC* MAGAZINE, APRIL 1971

Glaciers cover more than half of the Svalberg archipelago in the Norwegian Sea. Despite that, 2,500 people and 2,500 polar bears call this chain of islands home.

FRANCE

PROVENCE LAVENDER

"Perhaps no other scent so readily defines Provence than the pungent, heady aroma of lavender, and no other scene than the fields and fields of tiny purple buds growing in a profusion of mounds beneath an ultramarine summer sky. The first flowers appear in June, bursting forth in full glory by the end of the month in a hazy, violet-blue aura of beauty."

—BARBARA A. NOE, NATIONAL GEOGRAPHIC EDITOR AND AUTHOR

During summer, the southeastern French region of Provence is bathed in the sight and scent of lavender flowers. Various *routes de lavande* guide visitors through the region's fields and associated celebratory festivals. *Pictured:* The full moon rises . . .

Tony Hawk
Santorini, Greece

"[The] hotel ... looked too picturesque to be real ... so I muttered to my wife, 'I've never been to Greece.'"

I was peeking over my wife's shoulder at an email from our close friend requesting we go on vacation together. What followed was a link to a hotel website with images that looked too picturesque to be real. I noticed it was located on an island in Greece, so I muttered to my wife, "I've never been to Greece . . . ," and the ball started rolling.

We arrived in the heat of the summer. But the July skies were sparkling and the temperatures made the prospect of an island visit all the more appealing. On the way to Santorini, we spent a day like Griswold-type tourists in Athens. Which meant hiking in the hot sun to the top of the Acropolis with thousands of other tourists. As cliché as it seems, the view was stunning; all of Athens is laid out before you, with thousands of years of human history to gape upon.

With a few hours to kill, we decided to search out the legendary Skate House, a private home with a mini skate park inside. Through a series of emails and calls, we got in touch with the owner, a former skater who liked the aesthetic that ramps provided. We arrived five minutes later, moved her coffee table, and skated for 20 minutes, nearly hitting the flat-screen TV twice and falling into the bathroom after a misguided hand plant. It was just enough to get a short video clip: youtube/1FmQzAqKOY0.

We then flew to Santorini, a breathtaking flight in itself. We landed as the sun was setting, making the entire island glow in a golden hue.

On most travel sites, one of the top "things to do" in Santorini is "nothing." We took that advice for the most part, taking in the amazing views and Greek cuisine every day. We spent one day on a boat, exploring the island and visiting the hot springs. Santorini is essentially what's left of a huge volcanic eruption 3,600 years ago that is the basis of Atlantis folklore. But if Atlantis is an undiscovered paradise under the sea, Santorini is the terrestrial—and real—counterpart.

I highly recommend a trip there, especially in summer when you can experience clear skies and warm water. Once you arrive, do nothing as fast as possible, except cooling off in the beautiful Aegean Sea.

Tony Hawk is arguably the world's most famous professional skateboarder and founder of the Tony Hawk Foundation.

Get on the fast track to lazy days in Santorini—where "sit in hot springs" and "eat local cuisine" are a reasonable day's to-do list.

KENYA
LAKE NAKURU

"The waters of Lake Nakuru aren't blue, nor do they shine gold or silver under the African sun. The lake is pink, a shifting, standing, flying, fluttering mass of hundreds of thousands of flamingos that feed here, a bird-watcher's paradise that the park's warden calls 'a chance to see God through His creation.'"

—GRAEME GREEN, NATIONAL GEOGRAPHIC WRITER

Located in central Kenya, the shoreline of Lake Nakuru is home to millions of flamingos. The prevalence of algae growing in this salty lake attracts a wide variety of species.

The Spier Estate's Mojo restaurant pairs some of the Cape Winelands' stellar vintages with a shady alfresco setting.

SOUTH AFRICA

CAPE WINELANDS

Soak in mountain landscapes while sipping on wine with a 350-year history.

Sheltered by lush mountains and nourished by rich valleys, the Cape Winelands region is steeped in a multitude of soil types perfect for grapevines, allowing South African winemakers to become some of the most prolific in the world. Though the first vines were planted just outside Cape Town in 1655, today the heart of wine country beats about an hour's drive east. Surrounding the towns of Stellenbosch, Franschhoek, and Paarl are hundreds of wineries, many located on centuries-old estates, where gabled mansions with bright white facades stand out against craggy, mountainous backdrops.

The region is linked via multiple wine routes that meander through rolling farmland. Arrive from late July to mid-September, as South Africa's winter dissolves into spring and the vines come to life with new growth. That way, you'll be surrounded by flowers under fresh, springlike skies instead of the crowds that populate the region during the hotter January to April summer months.

CYCLE THE VINEYARDS OF STELLENBOSCH

Start out in Stellenbosch, where tree-shaded streets are lined with some of the most iconic examples of Cape Dutch architecture in South Africa—clean, whitewashed gables

Surrounding the towns of Stellenbosch, Franschhoek, and Paarl are hundreds of wineries, many located on centuries-old estates, where gabled mansions with bright white facades stand out against craggy, mountainous backdrops.

Savor Zorgvliet Wine Estate's Sauvignon Blanc in the tasting room housed in a building from 1692 or, better, in a room at their lodge.

GREAT BARRIER REEF

"Soft corals top hard ones, algae and sponges paint the rocks, and every crevice is a creature's home. The biology, like the reef, transforms from the north—where the reef began—to the south. The shifting menagerie is unmatched in the world."

—JENNIFER S. HOLLAND, *NATIONAL GEOGRAPHIC* MAGAZINE, MAY 2011

One of the seven wonders of the natural world, the Great Barrier Reef, located off the north-eastern coast of Australia, comprises more than 3,000 individual reefs and covers more than 134,360 square miles (348,000 sq km) of the Coral Sea. *Pictured:* A pink anemonefish peeks out from its sea anemone host.

FALL

HOT-AIR BALLOONING, BLAZING FOLIAGE, VIBRANT WILDFLOWERS, AND AN OKTOBERFEST OR TWO

Autumn color explodes in the vineyards of the Douro Valley, Portugal.

ALBUQUERQUE, NEW MEXICO

INTERNATIONAL BALLOON FIESTA

"Every October, magic comes to Albuquerque as hundreds of colorful and whimsical hot-air balloons silently soar into the clear blue New Mexico morning. They fill the sky like brightly patterned ornaments. On the ground, adults and children wander among the rising behemoths, craning their necks and waving at the balloonists and saluting their adventurous spirit."

—NEALA SCHWARTZBERG, JOURNALIST AND EDITOR

The International Balloon Fiesta occurs annually in the first week of October at Balloon Fiesta Park in Albuquerque, New Mexico. Since its genesis in 1972, the festival has grown exponentially in size from 13 to more than 600 balloons.

VACATION WITH ICE BEARS
Boyd Matson
Churchill, Manitoba

Polar bears are like the supermodels of the Arctic, used by advertisers to sell everything from sodas to hybrid cars. As ubiquitous as their image is, most people never get a chance to see real live polar bears in the wild, because they live primarily in isolated, hard-to-get-to places. However, there's one place where, every fall, you're almost guaranteed a sighting—lots of them: Churchill, Canada.

The first time I went to Churchill, I was working with leading bear biologist Malcolm Ramsay. We had darted two polar bears and were taking measurements for his research when Malcolm pointed to his assistant and noted that he is the "world's foremost expert in polar bear posteriors." I turned to see his arm inserted halfway up the bear's backside, collecting a stool sample. At that moment I said, "I've never wanted to be that much of an expert about anything."

Fortunately, it's not necessary to be a posterior expert, or a bear researcher of any kind, to get a close-up look at polar bears in Churchill. The town bills itself as the "polar bear capital of the world," and every autumn the bears show up to welcome visitors like chamber of commerce greeters. Churchill is where the ice first forms on Hudson Bay, and these bears love ice, because it means they can finally eat after a summer of fasting. They start arriving in October eagerly awaiting the first freeze. By Halloween, there are so many bears around town, armed guards go out to protect the trick-or-treaters.

When I went back to Churchill as a tourist one November, we went out in tundra rovers, big buslike vehicles on giant five-foot-tall (1.5 m) tires. It insured I was both safe and warm, while I was still able to get amazing close-up pictures of the bears from three feet (1 m) away. I also spent three nights in the Tundra Buggy Lodge to avoid missing any action while driving back and forth to town. Staying at the lodge enabled me to go to sleep and wake up with polar bears. To make the experience even more memorable, one night there was also a stunning light show courtesy of the aurora borealis. Best of all, no one had to be an expert or get their hands dirty for these close encounters.

Boyd Matson is a journalist and adventurer for National Geographic. He hosts the radio show National Geographic Weekend *and is a contributing editor for* National Geographic Traveler *magazine.*

"Staying at the [Tundra Buggy] lodge enabled me to go to sleep and wake up with polar bears."

A polar bear and her cub walk across the thick ice that coats Hudson Bay.

PENNSYLVANIA
HAWK MOUNTAIN

"Since 1934, more than a million people have visited Hawk Mountain sanctuary to watch the spectacular autumn flyby of 16 species of raptors, including Cooper's hawks, golden eagles, and merlins. Looking a hawk in the eye and seeing the individual feathers in its wings gives you a brief glimpse of its wild magnificence."

—RACHEL J. DICKINSON, *NATIONAL GEOGRAPHIC TRAVELER*
MAGAZINE WRITER

Every fall, the changing weather requires hawks to migrate south for the winter in search of food. Hawk Mountain, in Kempton, Pennsylvania, is one of the best places to observe this migration, with about 18,000 hawks passing through each fall.

GREAT HALLOWEEN HAUNTS

Get totally spooked at these perfectly ghastly haunts.

THE STANLEY HOTEL
Estes Park, Colorado

At this Rocky Mountains hotel, people claim that ghosts tuck them in at night and play piano in the music room. The Stanley helped inspire Stephen King's *The Shining,* and today you can sleep in the suite that's named for him. Just be sure to book far in advance.

www.stanleyhotel.com

LEMP MANSION
St. Louis, Missouri

This Victorian mansion boasts lovely hand-painted ceilings, stately mahogany mantles . . . and a history of untimely deaths and suicides. Now an inn, it hosts paranormal tours. The mansion sits above caves and tunnels once used for the family brewery business. Visit the brewery for Halloween, when the caverns are splattered with "blood" and you can descend into a subterranean haunted house.

www.lempmansion.com, www.scarefest.com

EASTERN STATE PENITENTIARY
Philadelphia, Pennsylvania

Resembling a medieval fortress, Eastern State Penitentiary isolated prisoners to the point of madness. The last inmate left in 1971, and tourists now walk the crumbling cell blocks, some reporting ghostly screams. Every fall, the 180-year-old prison hosts a punishing haunted house.

www.easternstate.org

TOWER OF LONDON
London, England

A place where queens were beheaded and young princes mysteriously disappeared, the Tower of London is steeped in tragic stories with gruesome outcomes. Today, Yeomen Warders, aka Beefeaters, lead twilight tours, taking visitors across cobblestone pathways and up spiral staircases after hours—when the Tower feels deathly quiet.

www.hrp.org.uk/toweroflondon/whatson/towertwilighttours

EDINBURGH CASTLE
Edinburgh, Scotland

From an accused witch burned at the stake to a headless drummer, ghosts have been reported at Edinburgh Castle for hundreds of years. Some visitors say they've felt burning sensations and seen shadowy figures in the 12th-century Scottish fortress that towers over the Scottish capital.

www.edinburghcastle.gov.uk

BARDI CASTLE
Bardi, Italy

A tragic legend of love haunts this northern Italian castle. He was a captain; she, the daughter of a lord. She saw enemy knights approaching, assumed her love had died in battle, and leapt from a tower. He was, in fact, donning enemy colors to celebrate victory. When he found his dead love, he killed himself, too. People say his ghost still searches for her.

turismo.comune.parma.it

HOUSKA CASTLE
Blatce, Czech Republic

Built over a gaping crack in the ground, Houska Castle blocked a deep gateway to hell, according to local legend. Rumors say the 13th-century Gothic castle hosts a bleeding headless horse and a roaming gloomy figure called the "white lady." The chapel sits directly over the caverns, allegedly to prevent underworld demons from escaping.

www.ceskolipsko.info/dr-en/1230-houska-castle.html

GOOD HOPE CASTLE
Cape Town, South Africa

Built by soldiers and slaves in the 17th century, Good Hope Castle didn't live up to its name for its dungeon's prisoners. Within the pentagonal fortress, torture was often used to extract confessions. Listen carefully: Some claim they still hear the screams of anguished souls.

www.castleofgoodhope.co.za

BHANGARH
Rajasthan, India

Was this abandoned fortress and village in northern India cursed by a lovestruck tantric who didn't get his way? Or doomed by an arrogant king? Even if you prefer the more mundane explanations of drought and war, it's easy to sense why the ornate but crumbling 16th-century ruins are the source of myriad tales of hauntings.

www.rajasthantourism.gov.in/destinations/alwar/bhangarh.aspx

MONTE CRISTO
Junee, Australia

A woman known to dress in high-collared black lace dresses is said to stalk this sprawling Victorian homestead in southeastern Australia. If you book a bed-and-breakfast ghost tour, the management suggests you come equipped with a flashlight—and that you arrive "prepared to be scared."

www.montecristo.com.au

Edinburgh Castle is rumored to
have more than enough ghosts—
including a "witch" who was
burned at the stake—to unsettle
even the biggest doubters.

NEW YORK
FALL FOLIAGE

"When people think of autumn in upstate New York, they usually think of a snapshot, not a succession. But a succession it is. The maples with their feet in the water redden and vanish first. Then come the dry-ground maples and the hickories, the hardwoods that seem to set the hills on fire. And when they're gone, the oaks remain, which light up the hollow, blank woods of November."

—VERLYN KLINKENBORG, AUTHOR AND *NEW YORK TIMES* CONTRIBUTOR

The spectacular fall foliage of upstate New York peaks in September and October. The Adirondack Mountains are an ideal and well known spot to view the shock of autumnal colors, attracting thousands of visitors a year. *Pictured:* Adirondack Park's High Peaks region

CAPITAL TALES

Cokie Roberts
Washington, D.C.

The Library of Congress National Book Festival celebrates a bibliophile's dream lineup of authors, poets, and illustrators.

Ah, late summer in Washington—the time to schedule that trip to the nation's capital. No, I'm not kidding, despite the weather's rotten reputation. In late September (technically the first days of fall, but hot days have a way of ignoring the calendar in this city) tents pop up on the National Mall, bracketed by the United States Capitol at one end, the Washington Monument at the other. In that great ceremonial space for two days you can hear people . . . reading—yes, reading and talking about books at the National Book Festival.

Then First Lady Laura Bush introduced this excellent addition to the capital's calendar in 2001, working with the longtime head of the Library of Congress, Jim Billington. Mrs. Bush felt certain that people would actually show up to listen to authors, ask them questions, stand in line for their signatures, and buy their books. She guessed right: Hundreds of thousands now celebrate the festival, even when it rains.

And if readers love it, authors love it even more. The first year I participated, I was stunned to find my tent stuffed to the flaps with people eager to hear more about women in American history, women who would be amazed to see how nicely the capital city they first settled has grown up. History's a natural subject for this spot, but there's a genre for everyone: mystery writers, cookbook chefs, novelists. Jules Feiffer came one year, Heloise another.

Sports figures draw crowds, but so do children's book authors. That's one of the great things about this festival—it's a family affair. Kids jab and jostle each other to get closer to their favorites, spellbound by Rick Riordan, titillatingly terrified by R. L. Stine, cracked up by Mo Willems.

For the 1,200-plus volunteers who help staff the complex event, it's all about getting kids into the tents, literally and figuratively. Watching youngsters listen and learn and then pester their parents into buying a *book* makes the sometimes sweaty work worth it. And once kids get hooked, they beg to come back year after year. I know. When his mother was busy one year, my grandson announced confidently, "Cokie will take me." And so I did, happily.

Cokie Roberts is a political commentator for ABC News and National Public Radio. She has appeared at the book festival several times to talk about her best-selling books and to accompany her grandchildren.

"I was stunned to find my tent stuffed to the flaps with people."

HARVEST FESTIVALS

Reap the rewards of a bountiful season with wine, food, song, and fun.

NIAGARA WINE FESTIVAL
St. Catharines, Ontario, Canada

Join the jubilant Pied Piper Parade through St. Catharines' Montebello Park before sampling the cool-climate vintages at on-site tastings. The two-week (typically late September) grape harvest celebration also includes free concerts, culinary events, a closing weekend Grand Parade, and excursions to the region's 80-plus wineries.

www.niagarawinefestival.com

SONOMA COUNTY HARVEST FAIR
Santa Rosa, California

With more than 250 wineries, Sonoma County, located 45 minutes north of San Francisco, is one of the world's premier winegrowing regions. At the county's annual October fair, all are welcome to mash their way into the World Championship Grape Stomp, sample wine from more than 150 wineries, and participate in hands-on farm activities.

www.harvestfair.org

NATIONAL APPLE HARVEST FESTIVAL
Arendtsville, Pennsylvania

Rural Adams County, Pennsylvania's largest producer of apples, holds its National Apple Harvest Festival the first two weekends in October. Thousands flock to the event, enticed by the aromas of homemade apple dumplings, fresh-pressed cider, and piping hot apple pies.

www.appleharvest.com

VENDIMIA FESTIVAL
Jerez de la Frontera, Spain

Throughout September, *vendimia* (harvest) fiestas are staged across Spain's winegrowing regions. Beginning on the weekend closest to September 8 (the Feast of the Nativity of Our Lady), head to Andalusia's sherry capital, Jerez de la Frontera, for one of the liveliest—a nonstop bullfighting/flamenco/dancing/grape-stomping fest.

www.andalucia.com

CANNSTATTER VOLKSFEST
Stuttgart, Germany

Stuttgart's annual beer and harvest festival lasts three weeks, from late September through early October. Massive brewery tents surround a decorative, eight-story "fruit column." Between sips of pilsner, ride the world's tallest mobile Ferris wheel and try traditional dishes like *Käsespätzle* (Swabian noodles with cheese).

www.cannstatter-volksfest.de

ALBA INTERNATIONAL WHITE TRUFFLE FAIR
Alba, Italy

Known as "white gold," the white truffles of northwest Italy's Piedmont region are prized for their near-garlic flavor and intoxicating aroma. Taste white-truffle-infused pasta, risotto, and sauces at Alba's annual fair, held every weekend from early October through mid-November. Festivities begin with traditional donkey races and a grand procession by more than 1,000 costumed locals.

www.fieradeltartufo.org

ST. LEOPOLD'S FEAST DAY
Klosterneuburg, Austria

The monks of Klosterneuburg Abbey, where founder and Austrian patron St. Leopold is buried, have been making wine for 900 years. Visit the abbey in the Vienna Woods on Leopold's November 15 feast day and celebrate with a carnival, music, and good luck slides down a huge wooden wine cask.

www.stift-klosterneuburg.at

MARUNADA FESTIVAL
Lovran, Croatia

Mid-October is sweet chestnut, or *maruni*, season along Croatia's Opatija Riviera. Historic, coastal resort Lovran kicks off the three-weekend festival before neighboring villages Liganj and Dobreć take a turn. Taste every imaginable chestnut-infused delight—from pancakes to sorbet—and then work off the calories in a bike race.

www.tz-lovran.hr

SUKKOT
Jerusalem, Israel

Called the "time of our joy," Sukkot celebrates fall's bounty while remembering how the Israelites were protected as they wandered the Sinai. Families build ceremonial, open-roofed huts, or sukkah, to eat (or even sleep) in for a week. Visit the massive sukkah erected on Jerusalem's Safra Square for free concerts, food fairs, and other joyful events.

www.gojerusalem.com

MOON FESTIVAL
Hong Kong, China

Held throughout Asia on the 15th day of the eighth month in the Chinese calendar (September or early October), the Hong Kong version of this harvest, family, and full-moon holiday is a high-voltage extravaganza with massive lantern sculptures and explosive fire dragon dances. See thousands of elaborate displays at Victoria Park's Lantern Wonderland.

www.discoverhongkong.com

It's all about the grapes at Jerez de la Frontera's September harvest festival in Andalusia, Spain—until the high-energy flamenco and bullfighting kick in.

OTHER OKTOBERFESTS

Bavarian bashes brew worldwide, allowing stein-lovers to celebrate . . . wherever.

KITCHENER-WATERLOO, ONTARIO, CANADA

Expect an authentic taste of Germany from a city that was named Berlin until 1916. Be transported by the merriment pouring from Kitchener's festival halls and filling steins, plates, and dance floors. Family-friendly events include blunt-tipped archery showdowns, a fashion show, and art gallery romps downtown before the Canadian Thanksgiving parade.

www.oktoberfest.ca

CINCINNATI AND COLUMBUS, OHIO

Lederhosen-clad locals, thirsty visitors, and even costumed racing dachshund pups raid six blocks of downtown "Zinzinnati" for one of America's most popular Oktoberfests—nearly 500,000 attendees strong. But the fairgrounds in Ohio's capital city of Columbus can't be overlooked, and you'll want to save room here for a half-pound cream puff from Schmidt's Restaurant und Sausage Haus.

www.oktoberfestzinzinnati.com, www.columbusoktoberfest.com

LEAVENWORTH, WASHINGTON

A Bavarian-style village in the foothills of the northern Cascade mountains brings in millions of thirsty visitors during the first three weekends of October. Don't miss the traditional keg-tapping ceremony by the small town's mayor kicking off each weekend.

leavenworthoktoberfest.com

COLONIA TOVAR, VENEZUELA

Called the "Germany of the Caribbean," this northern Venezuelan community an hour west of Caracas surprises with its unlikely Bavarian architecture and pride. The authentic culture lasts in the wake of immigrants from Germany's Black Forest who founded the town in 1843. Watch the trunk-sawing competition and enjoy a Tovar beer at one of the tables imported from Germany for the fest.

www.venezuelatuya.com

BLUMENAU, BRAZIL

Why not southern Brazil for Oktoberfest? This city is as authentic as many—it was founded in the mid-19th century by a small band of German immigrants. Try beers from local craft breweries such as Das Bier at Latin America's largest Oktoberfest celebration. Cut straight for the *biergarten* among the pavilions of Blumenau's expansive German Village Park reminiscent of Munich's own 14-tent grounds, or snag a freebie from the *bierwagen* parading the town.

www.oktoberfestblumenau.com.br

BANGALORE, INDIA

Leading Indian brewery Kingfisher throws an annual multi-stage music festival at the striking Jayamahal Palace in the heart of the southern Indian city. The musicians are bound to steal your attention, but the flea market is a highlight, too, complete with craft vendors and food stalls. More than 20,000 people attend the festivities each year.

www.kingfisherworld.com/tgiof

HONG KONG, CHINA

Not to miss out, this bustling Chinese island is home to a rollicking, annual *bierfest* at the Marco Polo Hongkong Hotel. Listen to traditional oompah bands and sample the roasted pork knuckle from your open-air perch over Victoria Harbour at this German/Asian tradition that's been going strong for more than 20 years. Get there early for one of the 200 pints of the exclusive Löwenbräu Oktoberfestbier served each night.

www.gbfhk.com/aj

DUBAI, UNITED ARAB EMIRATES

It's actually hard to miss Dubai's October salutes to old Bavaria with so many glittering venues around the city bedecked in German tinsel. A daylong bash is held in the Dubai Sports City complex, while area resorts such as the five-star Jumeirah Beach Hotel host their own. If you miss the October festivities, you can get a taste of Bavaria year-round at the Jumeira Rotana hotel's Brauhaus German Restaurant.

www.definitelydubai.com

BRISBANE, AUSTRALIA

Aussies get a balmy Oktoberfest experience on Queensland's east coast, where temperatures average 70°F (21°C) for this dual-weekend salute to Bavaria. And boasting a spread of entertainment from a Bavarian Strongman Competition and cowbell ringing to music, dancing, and a yodeler named Heidi, the event deserves a *prost* for still being family organized. And don't forget the beer: The festival imports its handcrafted brews from the old Tucher Brewery in Bavaria.

www.oktoberfestbrisbane.com.au

PORT ELIZABETH, SOUTH AFRICA

The German Club of Port Elizabeth might have a members-only beer garden, but it opens up its turf to the rest of Nelson Mandela Bay for one celebratory October weekend. The band Viva Bavaria plays classics from the Alps as well as classic rock and modern hits.

germanclub.co.za

Members of the Alpenrosen Dance Group raise their hats high as they twirl through some traditional moves at Brisbane, Australia's annual Oktoberfest.

Switzerland's orchards grow more than 600 varieties of apples, including Heimenhofer and Wildmuser.

EUROPE

SWITZERLAND

Pluck deliciously ripe apples among the autumn mists and picturesque orchards that dot the Swiss countryside.

Clean, picturesque, and law abiding, Switzerland is not the kind of place where you casually jump the fence to pluck a low-hanging Jonagold or Golden Delicious. Fortunately, the countryside is dotted with orchards where you can legitimately pick your own. During fall's harvest season, it is a grand day out.

In Versoix, a sleepy agricultural town overlooking Lake Geneva, rows of trees bulging with ripe red and yellow apples melt into the delicate outline of the Jura Mountains. In late September, families wander the sprawling groves of farms like Verger de Saint-Loup or Domaine de l'Orcy, intoxicated by the autumn mists and overwhelming choice. Switzerland has more than 600 traditional, largely forgotten apple varieties all its own for everyday munching or turning into dainty *tartes* or cider. The small-fry dart among the boughs in pursuit of the biggest, juiciest Mairac or Junami, leaving their parents to schlep 20-pound (9 kg) bags to the till. "You'll smile at your children picking their own fruit," says Geneva travel writer Michela Mantani. "It lets them try new foods without making a fuss."

The season reaches a festive climax in early October. Verger de Saint-Loup organizes a *fête de la pomme* (apple festival), with an apple-peeling contest and samples of freshly pressed juice.

PLANNING Apple-picking in Switzerland www.opage.ch. The apple harvest runs from September to mid-October. **Geneva** www.geneve-tourisme.ch.

BEST OF THE BEST
Gardens for the Stomach

A short drive north of Versoix, the town of Nyon and surrounds host some of the country's most fastidiously kept gardens—for vegetables, that is. From the leafy terrace of Nyon Castle, onetime home to the Savoy family and later the Bernese administration, a path zigzags through the municipal gardens of La Duche down to Lake Geneva. Board a short ferry to Yvoire and putter around the sumptuous Garden of the Five Senses, a green labyrinth complete with fountains, aviaries, and obscure medicinal herbs. Back in Nyon, visit the historic vegetable patch of beautiful Château de Prangins, where you discover ancient tubers that helped royalty survive those long, hard winters. www.myswitzerland.com

POLAND

MASURIAN LAKES

Catch the fall foliage reflected in the crystalline waters of a vast Eastern European lake system.

The secret has long been out on Poland's Masurian Lakes region in summer, but word is only starting to get around that the region makes a splendid autumn retreat as well. By late August, vacations have ended for summer revelers, and boat operators start to shutter. But a new season beckons with its open waters and changing shoreline scenery. Senses are heightened by the air's slight chill. The days—especially in September—are still warm enough for a comfortable afternoon out on the seemingly endless panorama of lakes—with some 2,000 to choose from. And by mid-month, the lakes' surrounding palette begins to turn fiery red and orange, shimmering in the crystal-clear reflection of the water's surface.

The Masurian chain of lakes, some interlinked by canal, begins 150 miles (240 km) northeast of Warsaw and stretches nearly to the Kaliningrad (Russia) and Lithuanian borders. The area once formed part of Germany's East Prussia and still retains a slight whiff of Teutonic sobriety.

In summer, ambitious kayakers set out on journeys that can last for weeks at a time and span several lakes, but in autumn, the tone is more subdued and the pleasures varied. Along with boating, get the blood flowing by hiking the leaf-strewn trails of the Masurian Landscape Park, a forest and biosphere that surrounds the waters.

PLANNING Masurian Lake District www.masurianlakedistrict.com. **Poland** www.poland.travel.

IN THE KNOW
The Wolf's Lair

Incongruously, only about 30 miles (48 km) from the beauty and tranquility of the Masurian Lakes stands what was arguably the epicenter of evil during World War II. It's here, in the former German region of East Prussia, that Adolf Hitler built his infamous command bunker, code-named Wolfs-schanze, or Wolf's Lair. The bunker was designed to house and hide the German leadership during their eastern attack on the Soviet Union. Visitors can tour what remains of the concrete structures and see the bunker where Hitler survived a 1944 assassination attempt led by one of his disgruntled officers, Col. Claus von Stauffenberg. www.wolfsschanze.pl

With the summer tourists gone, the crisp fall days at Lake Harsz in Masuria, Poland, make for a perfect retreat.

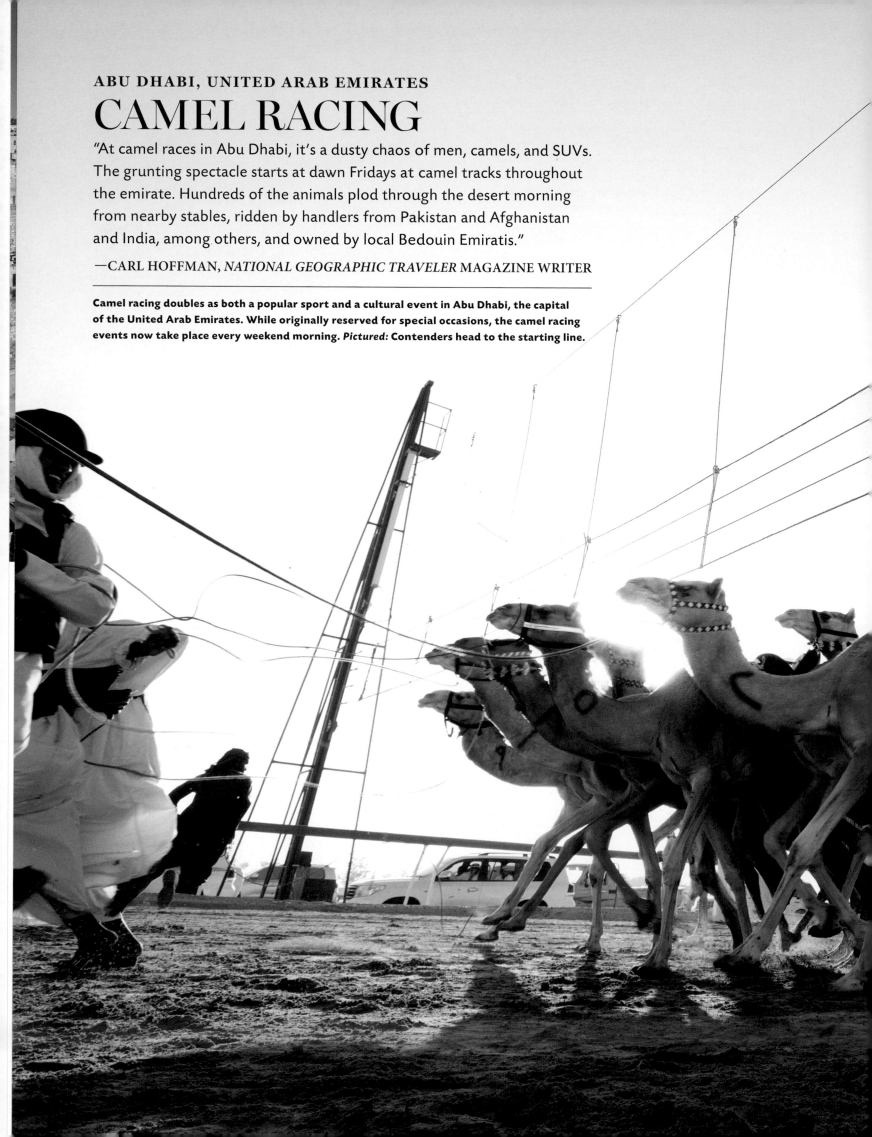

ABU DHABI, UNITED ARAB EMIRATES
CAMEL RACING

"At camel races in Abu Dhabi, it's a dusty chaos of men, camels, and SUVs. The grunting spectacle starts at dawn Fridays at camel tracks throughout the emirate. Hundreds of the animals plod through the desert morning from nearby stables, ridden by handlers from Pakistan and Afghanistan and India, among others, and owned by local Bedouin Emiratis."

—CARL HOFFMAN, *NATIONAL GEOGRAPHIC TRAVELER* MAGAZINE WRITER

Camel racing doubles as both a popular sport and a cultural event in Abu Dhabi, the capital of the United Arab Emirates. While originally reserved for special occasions, the camel racing events now take place every weekend morning. *Pictured:* Contenders head to the starting line.

A KALEIDOSCOPE OF AUTUMN LEAVES

Discover fabulous fall foliage the world over.

SONOMA COUNTY, CALIFORNIA

With leaves on both tree and vine, fall foliage is doubly intense in Sonoma County. Drive through Sonoma Valley along Arnold Drive, lined with multicolored canopies of oak and maple. Continue through the Russian River Valley, where vineyards paint the ground with sun-fire hues and wines are paired with the October squash harvests.

inside-sonoma.com

NORTHERN NEW MEXICO

In a state mischaracterized as a one-season desert, New Mexico's northern tip—which brushes the foot of the Rocky Mountains—beats to a seasonal rhythm. Drive the 83-mile (134 km) Enchanted Circle stretching from Taos to Red River, a diverse and scenic landscape of verdant valleys, cottonwood forests, and aspen-rimmed mountain lakes that turn to gold in late September and October.

www.enchantedcircle.org

HOLMES COUNTY, OHIO

In the heart of central Ohio's Amish Country, maple, oak, and the iconic state tree, the buckeye, hang over narrow roads that meander through wavy fields of corn. Drive under the boughs of bright reds and yellows, sharing the road with horse-drawn carriages of the Old Order Amish and stopping at roadside farm stands along the way.

fallinamishcountry.com

GASPÉ PENINSULA, QUEBEC, CANADA

Along coastal Quebec, maple leaves turn reds reminiscent of the leaf on Canada's flag. On the Gaspé Peninsula, the trees have the blue waters of the St. Lawrence Gulf as a backdrop. Hike the mountains of Parc National de la Gaspésie, or leaf-peep while whale-watching in Forillon National Park, where seven types of whales visit through October.

www.tourisme-gaspesie.com

DOURO VALLEY, PORTUGAL

Autumn transforms the Douro River Valley, which slices across northern Portugal, into a sea of red, orange, and yellow as the terraced vineyards that slope along the riverbanks prepare for winter. Take a cruise along the 125-mile (200 km) waterway, fortifying yourself against the autumn chill with a glass of the region's famed local port.

www.dourovalley.eu/en/

BAVARIA, GERMANY

Southern Germany is saturated with Alpine forests that pop with color against snow-dusted mountains. Meander along the 224-mile (360 km) Romantic Road, beginning in the Franconia wine region—where local wine festivals punctuate the autumn calendar—and heading south through centuries-old towns such as medieval Rothenburg ob der Tauber and Dinkelsbühl. Crowded with tourists in summer, fall offers more relaxed tempos for leaf-peeping.

www.romanticroad.com

TRANSYLVANIA, ROMANIA

Autumn breaks Count Dracula's spell in Transylvania, a place steeped in legend and imagery of sepia-toned medieval castles and hazy moonlight. Challenge yourself on the Transfăgărăşan, a 56-mile (90 km) drive through the Fagaras Mountains full of 90-degree turns, hairpin curves, and spectacular vistas of autumn's finest foliage.

www.romaniatourism.com

MOSCOW, RUSSIA

Moscow is defying its stereotype as a forbidding gray, Soviet-era metropolis and converting the estates of former tsars into public parks that paint the city with autumn hues. Try Kolomenskoye, where whitewashed palaces and blue, onion-shaped church domes punctuate a forest and rows of apple orchards.

mgomz.com

JIUZHAIGOU VALLEY, SICHUAN PROVINCE, CHINA

The Jiuzhaigou Valley hosts some of the most diverse flora and fauna in China. Autumn whips up a colorful competition between the dramatic red-orange leaves, rainbow-hued prayer flags of Tibetan villages, and emerald-tinged lakes that dot the landscape.

whc.unesco.org/en/list/637

KYOTO, JAPAN

In Japan, the leaf-viewing tradition—called *koyo*—mirrors its spring cherry blossom customs. One of the best spots for koyo is Kyoto on the island of Honshu, where vivid leaves frame sloping temple roofs, remnants of the city's many centuries of imperial history. Nighttime illuminations pierce the translucent, heavy branches at their colorful height from mid-November through December.

www.japan-guide.com

Hundreds of maples at Kyoto's Kitano Temmangu Shrine peak during autumn leaf season between November and mid-December.

MID-AUTUMN FESTIVAL

"It was like Halloween and Christmas combined . . . Downtown Hội An at night was loud and spectacular: There were dragons and lions and earth gods moved along by the kids inside . . . I walked down to the waterfront. Following everyone's example, I bought paper lanterns and boarded a small boat. I did what my fellow passengers did, lighting candles in these floatable lanterns and setting them free."

—JOSEPH HOBBS, DIRECTOR OF THE UNIVERSITY OF MISSOURI'S VIETNAM INSTITUTE

Tet Thrung Thu, the Mid-Autumn Festival, is celebrated across Vietnam. On the 15th day of the eighth lunar month, families and friends reconnect after the harvest. *Pictured:* **Festivalgoers set paper lanterns aglow.**

WIN

HOLIDAY LIGHTS, AURORA NIGHTS, COLD-WEATHER SPORTS, AND GETAWAYS SOUTH

TER

The northern lights cast an otherworldly glow over Bleik, Norway, a fishing village on the island of Andøya.

SCOTTSDALE, ARIZONA

NATIVE TRAILS FESTIVAL

"Native Trails is a collaboration of performing artists from Southwestern tribes in which we take the audience on a sensory journey, sharing our traditional and contemporary ways with instruments, regalia, food, song, and dance. While imparting our culture, we unite our energy, thereby encouraging a healthy outlook for future generations."

—DERRICK SUWAIMA DAVIS (HOPI/CHOCTAW),
NATIVE TRAILS ARTISTIC DIRECTOR

Scottsdale's Native Trails Festival runs from noon to 1 p.m. on most Thursdays and Saturdays between late January and early April at the Scottsdale Civic Center Park. *Pictured:* A traditional hoop dance

THE BAHAMAS
JUNKANOO

"Junkanoo is the ultimate Bahamian street party, celebrated throughout the islands on Boxing Day and New Year's Day. In Nassau, thousands of dancers don elaborate, brilliantly colored headdresses and costumes and parade down Bay Street to the music of cowbells and goatskin drums. It's a wild, joyful, utterly Caribbean festival."

—KAREN CARMICHAEL, NATIONAL GEOGRAPHIC WRITER

Junkanoo honors the freedom of African slaves. Starting at 2 a.m. on both December 26 and January 1, the festivities last until sunrise and include music, dance, and parades. *Pictured:* The streets of Nassau come alive for Junkanoo on New Year's Day, 2011.

MEXICO

MONARCH BUTTERFLY BIOSPHERE RESERVE

"The monarchs are everywhere. Hanging on the pines like flat Christmas ornaments and clumping like swollen beehives on the ends of branches. Some evergreens are so covered with butterflies that they resemble maples in the fall."

—MELINA GEROSA BELLOWS, *NATIONAL GEOGRAPHIC TRAVELER* MAGAZINE, NOVEMBER/DECEMBER, 2009

Falling temperatures trigger the beginning of the monarch butterflies' migration from the northern United States and Canada to their winter habitat at the Monarch Butterfly Biosphere Reserve near Mexico City. In the wintertime, millions of butterflies can be found in this UNESCO World Heritage site covering more than 138,000 acres (56,000 ha).

EASTER ISLAND
TAPATI RAPA NUI

"Decades ago the word 'compete' was defined as striving together, and the Rapa Nui festival on Easter Island embodies this concept wholeheartedly. With unique traditions such as racing down a 330-yard (300 m) hill on nothing more than a banana tree trunk, this old-school competition in the middle of the Pacific needs to be on your bucket list."

—YOGI ROTH, TV HOST, ACTOR, PRODUCER, AUTHOR, AND TRAVELER

Easter Island celebrates its Polynesian heritage with Tapati Rapa Nui, a two-week bash in February that blends traditional food, music, dress, and outdoor endurance events. The festival is inspired by and honors the heritage of the island. *Pictured:* A contestant in the banana tree slide

BOTTOM OF THE WORLD
Andrew McCarthy
Patagonia

I t used to be just sheep and gauchos. Now they come to El Calafate (population 7,000) from all over. Julia, who makes my smoothie at Viva La Pepa, moved down from Buenos Aires because she was "tired from the city." Jorge, who runs a bed-and-breakfast, came so he could "feel the sky." Even the old man with the gray mutt, who wears a black *boina* and sits all day on the bench on Avenida del Libertador, isn't local.

The January summer sun hovers in a sprawling sky. Then clouds roll in; rain pours down. Then the sun shines. Then it's raining again. Now the sun is out—all in 15 minutes. Sometimes the wind here blows so hard picnic tables roll like tumbleweeds. Small gray and white horses graze on long yellow grass while pink flamingos haul themselves up and fly off from glacier-milk lakes.

The gaunt lady who moved down from Rosario 11 years ago because "enough was enough" stares out at me from beneath long, dark bangs. She rents me a car and reminds me to park against the wind: "I don't need to have another door ripped off the hinges."

Down near the bottom of the world, the roads are narrow and empty, the vistas vast. Over a rise, the mammoth Perito Moreno glacier appears and glows, refracting light like a spaceship. When I step out onto the undulating, soaring, jagged ice, it crunches under the metal teeth of my crampons. Once I head back to town, I eat the largest and best steak of my life in a small and ugly restaurant.

A few hours up a deserted road, outside the village of El Chaltén, climbers from around the world appear like ants, clinging high up to the side of Mount Fitz Roy's sheer face. I hike the mountain's lower slopes. From a thorny bush, I pluck and nibble the blue-black calafate berry. Legend says that if a visitor eats one, he is sure to return—I grab another handful.

Andrew McCarthy is an actor, director, and editor at large for National Geographic Traveler *magazine. He is the author of the New York* Times *best-selling memoir* The Longest Way Home.

The spires, jagged peaks, and namesake glaciers of Los Glaciares National Park provide a dramatic frame around Lake Torre.

"Over a rise, the mammoth . . . glacier appears and glows, refracting light like a spaceship."

Alec Baldwin
Christmas in London

M y first trip overseas was to London. It was 1988. I was 30 years old. Having never traveled west of L.A. or east of St. Croix and being older than one normally might be for such a maiden voyage, I arrived at the Dorchester Hotel both wide-eyed and -eared. London meant the Tate, Turnbull & Asser, and Covent Garden—but London also meant, foremost, that inimitable sound: the British treatment of our nearly common language. And where better to hear that than in the temples built to celebrate the language in, perhaps, its highest form? So it was on to the theater to see Vanessa Redgrave in *A Touch of the Poet* and *Cat on a Hot Tin Roof* with Ian Charleson and Lindsay Duncan.

Londoners claim to have almost no relationship with sunshine, so winter is most familiar. Bundled up and uncomplaining, fireplaces and alcohol seem to replace zinc lozenges as protection from the effects of the cold. Eventually, Christmas in London became a nearly biannual tradition. Londoners adorn their city modestly for the occasion, so there were no giant plastic reindeer bobbing their heads, no unlicensed Santas marauding the airwaves to sell you credit card travel rewards (wink). And where that holiday summons images of cathedrals and choruses, the churches I tilted toward had names like the Olivier, the Royal Court, and Donmar Warehouse.

For Christmas 2007, my friend Jessica de Rothschild took me on a "tour" like no other of the London theater scene: *The Entertainer* at the Old Vic, Maggie Smith in *The Lady from Dubuque, Equus* with Daniel Radcliffe, and *Warhorse* at the National. We visited theater producers for lunch, ate dinner at J Sheekey or the Wolseley on Piccadilly. In between, I drifted off alone to the Garrick Club for Stilton cheese, Sautters on Mount Street for cigars, and Harrods to read the paper at the sushi bar.

London became an addiction, and thus fitting in those trips became more urgent. The Concorde, which once seemed foolish, became indispensable. And London at Christmastime, with its mix of solemnity, sarcasm, and the spoken word as an art form, became another home to me.

Alec Baldwin is a Golden Globe– and Emmy Award–winning actor and philanthropist.

London's famed Palace Theatre presents a stately visage for West End productions.

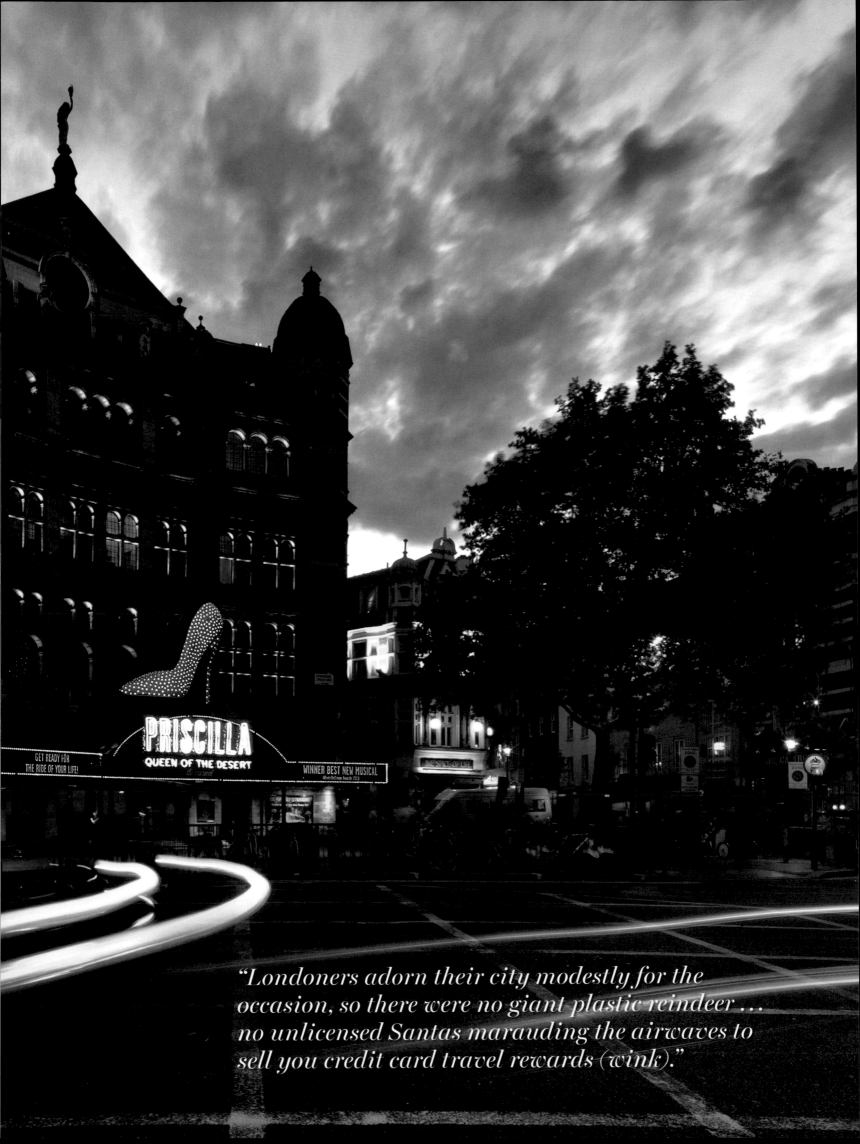

"Londoners adorn their city modestly for the occasion, so there were no giant plastic reindeer … no unlicensed Santas marauding the airwaves to sell you credit card travel rewards (wink)."

VALENTINE'S DAY RETREATS

Find cozy seclusion, starry views, ancient gardens—whatever your romantic heart desires.

POST RANCH INN

Big Sur, California

Perched on the Big Sur coastline, between the majestic Santa Lucia Mountains and the endless Pacific Ocean horizon, everything but the romance of the present moment is sure to fade away at the Post Ranch Inn. Choose from an array of ocean- or mountain-view accommodations, suites, or private houses, complete with outdoor hiking activities and relaxing spa amenities.

www.postranchinn.com

SEDONA

Arizona

Famous for its breathtaking red-rock landscape, Sedona is a prime spot for a secluded, romantic getaway. Take a sunset hike or horseback ride, or experience Sedona's rich viticulture with a tour of wine country in Verde Valley. Private canyon cabins, bed-and-breakfasts, and luxurious resorts are sprinkled throughout the area.

www.visitsedona.com

COVERED BRIDGES

Vermont

Known as "kissing bridges" back in the days of horse-and-buggy courtship, covered bridges provided a coveted moment of romantic privacy. A century later, these structures remain historic emblems of craftsmanship and are now a hallmark of picturesque New England. With more than 100 covered bridges, Vermont's scenic drives are the perfect reason for a bed-and-breakfast getaway.

www.visit-vermont.com/romantic-getaways

BRITISH PULLMAN TRAIN

United Kingdom

Step aboard British Pullman and transport back in time to the golden age travel of the 1920s. The sister train to the *Venice Simplon-Orient-Express,* the British Pullman celebrates the most romantic day of the year with a Valentine's Day tour through the British countryside. Featuring an elegant, locally sourced lunch or dinner, passengers enjoy cocktails and Champagne in luxury vintage carriages.

www.orient-express.com

HOTEL KAKSLAUTTANEN

Saariselkä, Finland

From the comfort of the Hotel Kakslauttanen's heated glass igloos, visitors sleep under a million-star canopy and the glowing northern lights. During the day, book a reindeer safari, sample from one of four restaurants, and relax in the world's largest smoke sauna.

www.kakslauttanen.fi/en

EIFFEL TOWER

Paris, France

Forgo the clichés and scale the Eiffel Tower to view fully the expanse of the most romantic city in the world. Stop on the second level for a cup of Parisian coffee and search the horizon for all the city monuments alongside your sweetheart.

www.eiffel-tower.com

THE LOVER'S WALK (VIA DELL'AMORE)

Cinque Terre, Italy

On the eastern shore of the Ligurian Sea lies one of Italy's most enchanting venues, Cinque Terre, comprising five villages etched into the salt-stained cliffs and connected by coastline paths. The pathway between Riomaggiore and Manarola, dubbed Via dell'Amore, provides breathtaking views of the turquoise sea and niches perfect for a romantic stroll.

www.cinqueterreriomaggiore.com

ISTRIAN PENINSULA

Croatia

Called the "Croatian Tuscany," the Istrian landscape abounds with rolling hills and valleys, hilltop villages, and patchwork expanses of wheat fields, vineyards, and olive groves. On February 14, couples will find a backdrop of snowcapped alpine mountains. View it all from above on a hot-air balloon ride.

en.gral-putovanja.eu

CLASSICAL GARDENS OF SUZHOU

China

Choose from dozens of exquisitely designed gardens dating from the 11th to 19th centuries—including the UNESCO World Heritage list–inscribed Lingering Garden and Couple's Garden Retreat—and wander arm-in-arm along winding paths and across elegant bridges.

www.china.org.cn

HA LONG BAY

Vietnam

Containing more than 1,600 islands, Ha Long Bay is a vision of astonishing beauty. Book an overnight cruise to watch the islands' limestone pillars, caves, and arches become steeped in rich oranges and purples at sunset and veiled in an ethereal morning mist at sunrise.

www.emeraude-cruises.com

The snowbound isolation of a log cabin at Inari, Finland's Hotel Kakslauttanen resort provides a very private Valentine's Day getaway.

VENICE, ITALY
CARNEVALE

"All the world repair to Venice to see the folly and madness of the Carnevale; the women, men, and persons of all conditions disguising themselves in antiq dresses, with extravagant musiq and a thousand gambols, traversing the streets from house to house, all places being then accessible and free to enter."

—JOHN EVELYN, ENGLISH DIARIST, 1646

In the 12 days leading up to Ash Wednesday, locals and visitors alike dress in brilliantly colored costumes and masks throughout Venice for Carnevale. *Pictured:* The city center, Piazza di San Marco, is home to many of Carnevale's main events.

HOT WINTER DRINKS

Warm up your chilly bones with the locals and experience culture in a cup
with these classic drinks, perfect for cold weather.

CRAFT COFFEE
Seattle, Washington

Starbucks served its first cup in 1971 from a quaint Pike Place Market café, spawning a Seattle coffee culture of artisan roasters and cafés. The Capitol Hill neighborhood offers the town's best brews, such as the two-story Caffè Vita, the flagship of an 18-year-old Seattle institution.
www.caffevita.com

YERBA MATE
Argentina

Argentines embrace this mainstay steeped beverage as a way to gather, slurping the earth-noted elixir from colorful, carved gourds through the same *bombilla,* or metal straw. Travelers can set out across the mate-producing regions on the Route of Yerba Mate to learn about the production process—from tree to gourd.
www.rutadelayerbamate.org.ar

WASSAIL
Somerset, England

Wassailing was originally a ritualistic English toast to healthy orchards marked by a January ceremony. The tradition continues in communities like those in the county of Somerset, where you can partake by dousing tree roots with cider and adorning limbs with bread—but save a cup of the wassail (hot cider) for yourself.
www.visitsomerset.co.uk

GRZANE PIWO
Krakow, Poland

Polish traditions rarely disappoint the taste buds, and *grzane piwo,* a seasonal mulled beer, is no exception. Just like wines or ciders in other places, the ale is heated, infused, and served. Plenty of pubs offer the hot brew, which complements a chilly day; try the patio at Glonojad Vegetarian Bar, flanking Matejki Square.
www.glonojad.com

GLOGG
Norway

Something heated, spiced, and/or spiked belongs on every winter menu, and for Scandinavians, glogg is a regionwide favorite. Usually it's made with hot red wine and zingy citrus and cinnamon, then spiked with spirit-soaked raisins. It can be mixed with hot (but never boiling) water or served as a straight shot.

ESPRESSO
Florence, Italy

Experiencing Italian café culture is as important as people-watching in the piazzas or admiring Renaissance masterpieces. The motherland of espresso has bragging rights to the potent little cup. Savor a buzzworthy shot at Caffè Scudieri's bustling espresso bar on Piazza San Giovanni.
www.scudieri.eu

HOT CHOCOLATE
Vienna, Austria

Wellsprings of culture, Vienna's ubiquitous coffeehouses create an aperture into everyday Viennese life. Hot chocolate is a sweet departure from the classic *kaffae,* especially when served the Austrian way: *mit schlag,* with whipped cream. The luxe Demel chocolatier offers its *schokolade* laced with ginger or cardamom, while Vienna's oldest coffeehouse, Cafe Frauenhuber, sticks to the chocolatey classic—mit schlag, of course.
www.demel.at, www.cafe-frauenhuber.at

MASALA CHAI
Kolkata, India

Shards of red clay cups linger around the bases of roadside stalls, and chai wallahs, or tea vendors, beckon passersby to add to the piles. This sweet-spiced milky comfort, also known as *chai karak,* steeps across India. In Kolkata, throwing empty cups against a wall or the ground is a tradition.

COFFEE CEREMONY
Addis Ababa, Ethiopia

An invitation to a traditional household coffee ceremony proves a sure sign of Ethiopian hospitality. The occasion includes green coffee bean roasting, hand-grinding, and steady refills. Savor the experience at Habesha Restaurant in the heart of Addis Ababa, or trek southwest to Jimma to see the quirky *jebena* coffeepot statue, oversized and overlooked by locals.
addisababaonline.com

PU-ERH TEA
Yunnan Province, China

Chinese tea porters used to traverse the 1,400-mile (2,250 km) Tea Horse Road swapping tea for horses in Tibet, and this dark, fermented tea got its name from a small trading post along the route. The most common kind, Pu-erh, develops a bitter flavor during the storage-fermentation process that soothes effects from oily foods.

Mexico bumps hot chocolate up a flavor notch by mixing in some heat with the sweet—and a side of dunk-worthy churros at the ready.

ZANZIBAR

Rock to sounds from all over the continent during a music festival on an idyllic East African island.

IN THE KNOW
The Irresistible Sounds of Taarab

As sunset descends on Stone Town in Zanzibar, the fabled island off the East African coast, you buy samosas and seafood kebabs from vendors in Foro-dhani Park and amble over to the ancient Old Fort. Inside, you stake your claim to a grassy patch near the main stage. But before you can finish your impromptu meal, you are dancing to the wildly varied sounds of the African mainland and Indian Ocean islands: desert soul from Mali, *marrabenta* from Mozambique, kora guitar virtuosos from Guinea.

It's one of the hottest times of year in equatorial Africa, but that doesn't stop people from moving to the rhythms at Sauti Za Busara, a February festival launched in 2004 that brings together dozens of established genres and fusion blends from all around the continent and beyond. The audience is equally eclectic. "It's quite something to be listening to a soul singer from Malawi, with a Maasai in full gear swaying next to you," says Zanzibar guidebook author Elizabeth Wollen.

Music is only part of the spectacle. Festivalgoers can watch dhow (sailboat) races, join a parade through the streets, browse handicrafts at the festival market, or even entertain the crowd at open-mic sessions where anyone is invited to sing.

PLANNING Zanzibar www.zanzibartourism.net. **Sauti Za Busara** www.busaramusic.org.

Freddie Mercury may be the best known singer from Zanzibar; the former Queen front man was born there in 1946. But the island's favorite music is *taarab*. Reflecting Zanzibar's multicultural heritage, taarab is a heady blend of Middle Eastern, European, and Indian influences. The name comes from the word *tariba*, which means to be "moved" or "agitated" in Swahili. And that's exactly what taarab does—moves you to get off your bum and dance. Although it can be performed solo, taarab is best with a full orchestra of Western instruments like accordions, keyboards, and violins mixed with traditional African ouds and *qanuns*.

Hundreds of musicians and dancers from all over Africa and beyond inject Zanzibar's annual Sauti Za Busara festival with an infectious, genre-busting energy.

Mozambique's endless expanses of empty coastline and clear waters create a rare, beachy respite.

MOZAMBIQUE

BENGUERRA ISLAND

Lose yourself in endless stretches of empty beaches along emerald waters when tropical skies are clear and dry.

On Benguerra, an island in the Bazaruto Archipelago off Mozambique's southern coast, the horizon dissolves between translucent turquoise waters and an aquamarine sky. Silence characterizes the coastline, where cars are a rarity. And best, even in its high season (winter in the Northern Hemisphere), when the tropical weather is optimum—dry and not too hot—other people are largely absent, too.

Walking is the main mode of transportation on Benguerra—an activity best enjoyed in the evenings, after characteristic afternoon rains soften the seasonal humidity. The slow pace gives the senses time to process the vast expanse of undulating beach. "All you focus on is the amazing blue sea," says longtime traveler Christine Laciak. "The water is just beautiful and serene."

Fishing, of course, is big here. Try casting for deep-sea catches like marlin and tuna, common in the summer waters, or spend the afternoon alongside local fishermen who navigate dhows, their nonmotorized wooden sailboats. "There's nothing industrial about it," Laciak says. "Just 30 people out there, hand-hauling nets."

Watching for Benguerra's 140-plus bird species and diving are also popular, eco-oriented activities. The good news for the island's roughly 1,000 residents: The World Wildlife Fund recently designated it a "gift to the Earth" to help preserve its Indian Ocean waters and the community that depends on them.

PLANNING Benguerra Island www.mozambique.co.za. The island is accessible by boat from the mainland town of Vilanculos. Vilanculos International Airport services flights, most of which connect from Johannesburg and Maputo.

GREAT STAYS
Luxurious and Eco-Friendly Resorts

These resorts help you leave a relatively small footprint, even during Benguerra's "busier" December-to-March high season.

● **AZURA RESORT:** Private beach villas dot Benguerra's first resort, community-minded since inception, from employing island-based construction workers to hiring local staff. azura-retreats .com/benguerra

● **BENGUERRA LODGE:** Gorgeous villas with thatched roofs and beachside views. The lodge collaborates with members of the island community to initiate environmental conservation projects and donates part of its revenue to an island trust. www.benguerra.co.za

It's not all "big five" game in Tanzania's Serengeti National Park—meet a petite lilac-breasted roller.

KENYA/TANZANIA

THE SERENGETI

Witness herds of wildebeests, lions, and other animals thunder across the untouched Serengeti during their spectacular annual procession.

The Serengeti is a gargantuan, 12,000-square-mile (31,800 sq km) game ecosystem in the heart of African bush country, crossing the border of Kenya and Tanzania, inscribed on UNESCO's list of World Heritage sites, and still hunted on and inhabited by Maasai warriors. This is the Africa of *Out of Africa* and the very birthplace of the safari. If you're coming to Africa for animals, it doesn't get any better than this. Calving season, when the grasses are ripest, lasts from January to March and is the ideal time to visit.

A SPECTACLE OF GREAT GAME, BIG . . .

The Serengeti is arguably the continent's best spot to witness "big five" game—lion, leopard, elephant, rhino, and buffalo—although hippos, crocodiles, cheetahs, bush babies, and hundreds of others animals abound, too. Watching the cavalcade peel down dirt paths worn by animals of generations past is one of Earth's grandest parades and most mysterious natural wonders.

The rainstorm-scattered season is the best to see this mass migration, when more than 400,000 wildebeest calves are born in a two- to three-week, naturally synchronized period. The voyage kicks off in the Ngorongoro Crater area of Tanzania's southern

IN THE KNOW
Endangered Species of the Serengeti

Rhino numbers have plummeted as demand for their tusks has soared. In particular danger is the black rhinoceros, whose population continues to drop. Sadly, elephants are endangered now as well, as demand for ivory has threatened their survival. A glimpse of a wild dog, elusive animals that travel in packs, is considered so rare it's cause for news. Lovable, lanky cats, a delight to witness, are also among the animals at risk; the most vulnerable, the cheetah, roams expansive tracts of ever-disappearing flat, grassy savanna. A proposed highway system that cuts through the Serengeti threatens to destroy this animal's habitat.

Serengeti and bucks, charges, and grunts its way to the Maasai Mara reserve in lower Kenya. The journey is longer than 500 miles (800 km)—and not all the animals survive. A great way to guarantee seeing the sights and sounds of the Great Migration "is to stay at the private game reserves closest to the river crossing points," suggests Lewela Mwawaza, guide for Micato Safaris. "Taking a hot-air balloon or helicopter is even better."

. . . AND SMALLER

The awesome spectacle also includes the migration of two million other herbivores, everything from gazelles to zebras, that graze on Serengeti spring buds and young grasses and perch on rocky kopjes, pausing at watering holes and windswept plains, at times just a few arms' lengths away from you. The big game is the most obvious lure, of course, but many visitors return for up close photo encounters with Africa's gentler and lesser known species, like colorful lilac-breasted rollers, herds of shy giraffes, and umbrella thorn acacia trees that dot the landscape and have inspired visitors (and sundowner sippers—see sidebar) for generations.

Even for safari vets, watching the mass movement of Serengeti wildlife is thrilling. "Every year I show guests the annual migration," says Tom Lithgow, founder of Firelight Expeditions and Tanzania's Lupita Island resort, "I always look upon this saga with awe. No year is the same."

PLANNING **Serengeti migration tours** Many consider Micato Safaris *(www.micato.com)* the best tour operator. &Beyond *(www.andbeyondafrica.com)* also has a portfolio of incredibly located properties and is lauded for its warm, local guides, each equipped with an extraordinary knowledge of natural history.

FOR FOODIES
History of the Sundowner

U nlike most cocktails, the sundowner—a colloquial British term—is more about the where and when than the what. It can be any number of cocktails taken after completing a day's work—or, in the case of tourists, a day's game drive through the bush. But the drink must be experienced at sundown in Africa. It offers safarigoers not only a chance to unwind but also a moment to reflect on the greatness of this wild, vast landscape. Its name originates from the early 20th century and was popularized by such safarigoing imbibers as Ernest Hemingway, Karen Blixen (of *Out of Africa* fame), and Teddy Roosevelt.

Hundreds of thousands of wildebeest, joined by zebras and other animals great and small, make their annual pilgrimage across the Serengeti.

NEW YEAR'S EVE CELEBRATIONS

Chime in the New Year with festivities both large and small around the world on this intercontinental journey.

NEW YORK CITY, NEW YORK

New Year's Eve in New York's Times Square defines the evening for hundreds of millions around the globe who watch on television, wishing they were there. A million revelers squeeze into the city's neon epicenter where Broadway and Seventh Avenue come together, waiting for the Waterford crystal LED ball to drop from the former New York Times Building, for which the iconic square is named. It's an American tradition more than 100 years old.

www.nycgo.com

LAS VEGAS, NEVADA

Ring in the New Year casino style in kitschy Las Vegas, where fireworks blast over Paris Las Vegas, the MGM Grand, the Bellagio, and the array of other casino hotels on the famous Strip. The city buzzes with tens of thousands who come in for special concerts and performances with the biggest stars, until the sun comes up over the surrounding desert.

www.lvcva.com

RIO DE JANEIRO, BRAZIL

Réveillon, Rio's New Year's celebration, is one of the world's largest. Dressed in white like Candomblé priestesses, millions of locals and visitors line the city's miles of beaches, throwing flowers into the waves at midnight for the African sea goddess Yemanjá, whose traditions have become mixed with the Virgin Mary. Afterward, the streets, bars, and restaurants fill with parties, dancing, and music.

www.rcvb.com.br

LONDON, ENGLAND

Millions of eager Londoners line the Thames waterfront and gather in Trafalgar Square, waiting for the city to explode in a dazzling display of sparks and color. At midnight, the tower around Big Ben pulses with fiery blasts timed for the 12 strokes of the hour. All eyes then turn to the London Eye as the famous wheel produces a swirling fireworks and light show timed to British rock music echoing through the city.

www.visitlondon.com

PARIS, FRANCE

The City of Light becomes a city of fireworks on New Year's Eve. Hundreds of thousands line the Champs-Élysées, Champagne bottles in hand, for a view to the Eiffel Tower. At midnight, fireworks burst from the entire length of its iron structure, in one of this evening's most beautiful displays anywhere. Other gathering spots with great views include the steps of Sacré-Couer church and the Trocadéro.

en.parisinfo.com

MADRID, SPAIN

Madrileños celebrate the new year by swallowing 12 grapes—1 for each stroke of the clock at midnight. Finishing them on time is considered to be a sign of good luck in the upcoming year. Tens of thousands gather in front of the clock in Puerta del Sol plaza for the annual ritual and line Gran Via to watch fireworks.

www.spain.info

BEIRUT, LEBANON

Each New Year's is a promise that everything will be better in the capital of formerly war-torn Lebanon. Thousands gather to watch the light show on the city's 1933 art deco clock tower in Nejmeh Square, the heart of central Beirut. At midnight, couples kiss and fireworks burst, shining over a mix of floodlit church steeples and mosque minarets in this eclectic Levantine metropolis.

www.lebanon-tourism.gov.lb

TOKYO, JAPAN

On New Year's Eve in Tokyo, streets and restaurants teem with people, many eating buckwheat noodles to ensure health and happiness in the New Year. Temples ring bells as a countdown to midnight, adding a dreamy quality to the celebration. Stay in town through January 2, one of only two days when the emperor opens the palace grounds to the public.

www.gotokyo.org/en

CHRISTMAS ISLAND, SOUTH PACIFIC

Named after another holiday (and famed as the likely location of Amelia Earhart's missing airplane), Christmas Island, or Kiritimati (in the South Pacific republic of Kiribati), is among the first inhabited places in the world to celebrate the New Year. With only around 5,000 residents, New Year's Eve is an intimate affair, much of the island being a protected wildlife sanctuary.

www.shire.gov.cx

SYDNEY, AUSTRALIA

Everyone comes to the waterfront in Sydney to celebrate New Year's Eve. The iconic Sydney Harbour Bridge and nearby buildings ignite at midnight with one of the world's most spectacular fireworks productions.

www.sydneynewyearseve.com

The Sydney Opera House, usually the focal point for visitors to the harbor, plays second fiddle to the New Year's fireworks display.

ICE MUSIC

Paul D. Miller, aka *DJ Spooky*
The Antarctic Peninsula

Whosoever will be an enquirer into Nature let him resort to a conservatory of Snow or Ice.—Francis Bacon

The universe, according to most scientists, has been around for about 13.7 billion years. Although Antarctica has been in existence for only about 60 million of those years, it still is a place to measure the tempo of the world and the alterations occurring because of massive climate change. Match one rhythm to the other and see what beats you can mix.

OK, so here I am in the Antarctic Peninsula, creating a series of drafts for several compositions that I'll eventually turn into string quartet pieces, a gallery show, and a symphony out of the experience. I'm looking at how to collect impressions of the landscape, distill the material into something that I can use in the compositions (visually, sonically, and for writing as well), and arrive at a point where sound and art can create portraits of what's going on down here.

The next couple of steps are about how this all comes together. DJ culture is all about collage—sampling, splicing, dicing, etc., etc.; everything is part of the mix, and there are no boundaries between sound sources. There's a lot of room for mapping sampling techniques to the environment itself. The world is a very, very, very big record. We just have to learn how to play it.

My excursion to Antarctica was a journey into the realm of the hypothetical, a world where fictions clash with the realities of the everyday world. Music is a mirror we hold up to society to see what derives from tone, pitch, and sequence. Antarctica is a place at the edge of the map, but we are aware of its deep reflections in how it regulates the tempo of the planet, the rhythm of the seasons. I just thought I'd give the idea a spin.

Paul D. Miller, aka DJ Spooky, is a composer, multimedia artist, editor, and author. In 2012–2013, he was the first artist-in-residence at New York's Metropolitan Museum of Art. LEFT: Original artwork by DJ Spooky.

"My excursion to Antarctica was a journey into the realm of the hypothetical, a world where fictions clash with the realities of the everyday world."

Currently free of government and development, Antarctica and its Holtedehl Bay remains the domain of ice floes, mountains, clouds, and sky.

NEW ZEALAND

MARLBOROUGH SOUNDS

Trek along the South Island's skyline ridges to hidden bays and tranquil coves in a coastal wonderland.

The intricately etched, sea-drowned valleys of the South Island's Marlborough Sounds make up a fifth of New Zealand's coastline. From the heights of the Queen Charlotte Track, gaze across dappled emerald ferns that descend to turquoise waters sparkling under February summer sunlight, when temperatures range from 68°F to 78°F (20°–26°C) here in the country's brightest region.

Start the trail at Ship Cove at the head of Queen Charlotte Sound, one of New Zealand's most historic sites and beloved by Captain Cook. "So glowing were Cook's comments around this area, his favorite place, that for the next 50 years the English thought of New Zealand in terms of his description of Queen Charlotte," says Malcolm Campbell, a New Zealand naturalist and National Geographic expert.

Today, some 240 years later, the still rather isolated area holds the same allure, with its sparkling waters, remote inlets, stunning coastal trails, and rugged bush. Campbell adds, "My most memorable trip was walking by day and spending the evenings staying on a converted North Sea fishing vessel, eating fresh seafood from the area, and sampling the local wines in the evenings, swimming in the mornings, hiking each day, meeting, and sharing the good company of like-minded people that we met along the track."

PLANNING Marlborough Sounds www.newzealand.com/int/marlborough-sounds. The Marlborough Sounds Adventure Company *(www.marlboroughsounds.co.nz)* offers guided hiking, mountain biking, and sea kayaking trips in the Sounds.

IN THE KNOW
Steeped in the Maori: Te Tau Ihu

The Maori call the northern end of the South Island Te Tau Ihu, "the prow" of the demigod Maui's canoe. With eight recognized *iwi*, or tribes, in the Nelson-Marlborough region, the area is steeped in Maori culture both ancient and modern. Visit *marae* (community gathering places) such as the one in Waikawa, outside Picton, where warriors will perform a *hongi*—the pressing of noses—before welcoming you into the carved meetinghouse for singing, dance presentations, and a shared meal. www.waikawamarae.org.nz

Trekkers along the edge-of-the-world Marlborough Sounds take in vistas both breathtaking and remote.

Adult and chick emperor penguins prep for a swim in Antarctica's Davis Sea.

THE ANTARCTIC

ANTARCTICA

Tuck into an on-deck BBQ and gaze at the penguins paddling by.

It's been almost 100 years since the explorers of the Heroic Age—Amundsen, Scott, Shackleton—took on the challenge of reaching the South Pole, some of their team members dying in the process. But the vast, pristine "white continent" of Antarctica, one of the world's last great wildernesses, hasn't lost its power.

Antarctica's summer, from December to March, is the best time for visitors. During these months, encounter whales and penguins at play in the relative warmth of Earth's southernmost sunlight.

Sunniva Sorby, a member of the first all-female team to walk to the South Pole without dogs, extols the "shared sense of living" one experiences: "The Antarctic illuminates the isolation, the desolation, the reflection of who you are as a person."

Unlike those early expeditions, cruise ships now provide safe and easy land and water excursions. After a hike up snowy hills scattered with noisy penguin rookeries or a raft ride among electric blue icebergs to spot whales and seals, recharge your batteries with a warm, hearty barbecue back on deck. Reggae music and sizzling burgers might feel incongruous, but mulled wine feels suitably wintry. The only likely interruption? Having to rush to the railings to watch whales, sea lions, or penguins swim by.

PLANNING Antarctic Cruises www.oneoceanexpeditions.com, www.quarkexpeditions.com, www .oceanwide-expeditions.com, www.nationalgeographicexpeditions.com. Most ships depart from Ushuaia at the southern tip of Argentina.

GREAT STAYS
Ice Camping

When the raft drops you on the snow-covered banks with a shovel, sleeping bag, and bivy sack for the night, there may well be thoughts of, What have I got myself into? And that's *before* the digging starts of your "snow grave" that will serve as a bed for the night. There's no mattress, room service, or central heating, but camping overnight in the Antarctic snow is an unforgettable experience and a tiny hint of what Amundsen, Scott, and company went through here. Several companies feature camping options, including Oceanwide Expeditions (*www .oceanwide-expeditions.com*).

CALENDAR OF EVENTS

SPRING

- SOUTH BY SOUTHWEST FESTIVAL, AUSTIN, TEXAS: mid-March (pp. 20–21)
- HOLI FESTIVAL OF COLORS AND ELEPHANT FESTIVAL, JAIPUR, INDIA: after the first full moon in March (pp. 72–73)
- SAN JUAN CAPISTRANO SWALLOWS, CALIFORNIA: March 19 (p. 12)
- SPRING EQUINOX AT THE PYRAMID OF THE SUN, MEXICO CITY, MEXICO: March 20 (p. 34)
- SUMO WRESTLING GRAND TOURNAMENTS, OSAKA AND TOKYO, JAPAN: March and May (p. 76)
- HOLY WEEK: last week of Lent (León, Nicaragua, p. 31; Seville, Spain, p. 60)
- TIN PAN SOUTH SONGWRITERS FESTIVAL, NASHVILLE, TENNESSEE: early April (p. 15)
- TULIP FESTIVAL, ISTANBUL, TURKEY: late March through mid-April (pp. 62–63)
- MASTERS TOURNAMENT, AUGUSTA, GEORGIA: first full week in April (p. 25)
- KING'S DAY, AMSTERDAM, THE NETHERLANDS: April 27 (p. 42)
- VERMONT MAPLE FESTIVAL, ST. ALBANS, VERMONT: late April (p. 22)
- SAILING WEEK, ANTIGUA: end of April to early May (p. 30)
- NEW ORLEANS JAZZ AND HERITAGE FESTIVAL, NEW ORLEANS, LOUISIANA: last weekend of April through first weekend of May (p. 19)
- MAY DAYS, KIEV, UKRAINE: May 1–9 (pp. 74–75)
- GIRONA FLOWER FESTIVAL, GIRONA, SPAIN: May 7–15 (pp. 58–59)
- WORLD CHAMPIONSHIP BARBECUE COOKING CONTEST, MEMPHIS, TENNESSEE: mid-May (p. 18)
- ROMANY PILGRIMAGE, SAINTES-MARIES-DE-LA-MER, FRANCE: May 24–25 (pp. 52–53)
- INDIANAPOLIS 500, INDIANAPOLIS, INDIANA: last weekend of May (pp. 16–17)
- GRAND PRIX, MONACO: late May (p. 45)
- FLAG DAY AND NEW HERRING AUCTION, SCHEVENINGEN, THE NETHERLANDS: early June (p. 43)
- FEZ FESTIVAL OF WORLD SACRED MUSIC, FEZ, MOROCCO: early June (p. 66)
- BLOOMSDAY, DUBLIN, IRELAND: June 16 (p. 38)

GENERAL SPRING DESTINATIONS AND ACTIVITIES

Craters of the Moon, Idaho (p. 13)
Theodore Roosevelt National Park, North Dakota (p. 14)
White-water rafting, West Virginia (p. 23)
Wine festivals, Virginia (p. 24)
Great Smoky Mountains, Tennessee/North Carolina (pp. 26–27)
Snuba, Puerto Rico (p. 28)
St. Lucia, the Caribbean (p. 29)
Cacao harvests, Ecuador (p. 35)
Guatemala Highlands, Central America (pp. 36–37)
Loch Lomond, Scotland (p. 39)
Wadden Sea National Park, Denmark (p. 44)
Paris, France (pp. 46–49)
Lake Como, Italy (pp. 54–57)
Bird-watching in the Danube Delta, Romania (p. 61)
St. Catherine's Monastery, Sinai Peninsula, Egypt (pp. 64–65)
Trekking in the Atlas Mountains, Morocco (p. 67)
Victoria Falls, Zambia/Zimbabwe (p. 70)
Shwedagon Pagoda, Yangon, Myanmar (p. 71)
Cherry blossom viewing, Japan (p. 77)

SUMMER

- WHITE NIGHTS FESTIVAL, ST. PETERSBURG, RUSSIA: weeks before and after the summer solstice, June 20/21 (p. 129)
- GOLFING UNDER THE MIDNIGHT SUN, ICELAND: mid- to late June (p. 115)
- INTI RAYMI FESTIVAL OF THE SUN, SACSAYHUAMÁN, PERU: June 20/21 (pp. 112–113)
- QUEENSTOWN WINTER FESTIVAL, QUEENSTOWN, NEW ZEALAND: late June (pp. 160–161)
- NATIONAL CHERRY FESTIVAL, TRAVERSE CITY, MICHIGAN: late June through early July (p. 95)
- PALIO, SIENA, ITALY: July 2 and August 16 (p. 137)
- INDEPENDENCE DAY ON THE NATIONAL MALL, WASHINGTON, D.C.: July 4 (p. 103)
- CALGARY STAMPEDE, CALGARY, ALBERTA, CANADA: early to mid-July (p. 88)
- HEIVA I TAHITI, TAHITI, FRENCH POLYNESIA: early to mid-July (p. 155)
- GREAT NORTHERN ARTS FESTIVAL, INUVIK, NORTHWEST TERRITORIES, CANADA: mid-July (p. 81)
- NAADAM FESTIVAL, ULAANBAATAR, MONGOLIA: July 11–13 (p. 152)
- LA FIESTA DE LA TIRANA, LA TIRANA, CHILE: July 16 (p. 110)
- JUST FOR LAUGHS FESTIVAL, MONTREAL, QUEBEC, CANADA: mid- to late July (p. 99)
- CHINCOTEAGUE PONY SWIM, ASSATEAGUE CHANNEL, VIRGINIA: last Wednesday of July (pp. 106–107)
- NEWPORT FOLK AND JAZZ FESTIVALS, NEWPORT, RHODE ISLAND: late July and early August (p. 102)
- HONDA CELEBRATION OF LIGHT, VANCOUVER, BRITISH COLUMBIA, CANADA: late July through early August (p. 80)
- SALZBURG FESTIVAL, SALZBURG, AUSTRIA: late July through August (p. 136)
- EDINBURGH FRINGE FESTIVAL, EDINBURGH, SCOTLAND: August (pp. 118–121)
- MEDIEVAL WEEK, GOTLAND ISLAND, SWEDEN: early August (p. 125)
- PERSEID METEOR SHOWER: August 11–13 (pp. 100–101)
- IOWA STATE FAIR, DES MOINES, IOWA: mid-August (p. 98)
- TANGO WORLD CUP, BUENOS AIRES, ARGENTINA: mid- to late August (p. 114)
- TELLURIDE FILM FESTIVAL, TELLURIDE, COLORADO: Labor Day weekend (p. 94)

GENERAL SUMMER DESTINATIONS AND ACTIVITIES

Bear viewing in Alaska (pp. 82–85)
San Juan Islands, Washington (pp. 89–91)
Pacific Crest Trail, California/Oregon/Washington (pp. 92–93)
Pawleys Island, South Carolina (p. 108)
Train ride through Copper Canyon, Mexico (p. 109)
Chapada Diamentina National Park, Brazil (p. 111)
Cornwall coast, England (p. 124)
Svalbard, Norway (pp. 126–127)
Cruise through the Baltic Sea (p. 128)
Parque Nacional Peneda-Gerês, Gerês, Portugal (p. 130)
Biking in the Pyrenees, France/Spain (p. 131)
Lavender fields, Provence, France (pp. 132–133)
Taking the waters at Switzerland's lakes and *badis* (pp. 134–135)
Santorini, Greece (page 140–141)
Opera in the Arena di Verona, Verona, Italy (p. 142)
Flood season in Okavango Delta, Botswana (p. 143)
Watching flamingos of Lake Nakuru, Kenya (pp. 144–145)
Seeing gorillas in the wild, Rwanda/Uganda/The Little Congo (p. 146)
Dune walking, Namibia (p. 147)
Cape Winelands, South Africa (pp. 148–151)
Beaches of Hong Kong, China (p. 153)
Climbing Mount Fuji, Japan (p. 154)
Great Barrier Reef, Australia (pp. 156–157)
Kakadu National Park, Australia (p. 158)
Skiing, Snowy Mountains, Australia (p. 159)

INDEX

Boldface indicates illustrations.

ILLUSTRATIONS CREDITS

Cover (clockwise from top left): Henry Georgi/Corbis, Smileus/Shutterstock; Johanna Huber/SIME; Design Pics/Corbis; 2-3, Michael Melford/NG Stock; 4, LOOK Die Bildagentur der Fotografen GmbH/Alamy; 6, Giovanni Simeone/SIME; 10-11, TAKASHI SATO/amanaimages/Corbis; 12, littleny/Shutterstock; 13, Dr. W. B. Karesh; 14, Don Johnston/All Canada Photos/Getty Images; 15, Will Van Overbeek/NG Stock; 16-7, William Manning/Corbis; 18, Randy Harris/Redux; 19, Amy Harris/Corbis; 20-21, ZUMA Wire Service/Alamy; 22, Robert F. Sisson/NG Stock; 23, Greg Von Doersten/Aurora/Getty Images; 24, Christy Massie/Courtesy of visit charlottesville.org; 25, Andrew Davis Tucker/Staff/the *Augusta Chronicle*/ZUMAPRESS. com/Alamy; 26-7, Visuals Unlimited, Inc./Adam Jones/Getty Images; 28, Vilainecrevette/Alamy; 29, Wildroze/iStockphoto; 30, Alison Langley/Aurora/Getty Images; 31, THALIA WATMOUGH/aliki image library/Alamy; 33, Hemis/Alamy; 34, Frans Lemmens/Hollandse Hoogte/Redux; 35, Owen Franken/Corbis; 36-7, holgs/iStockphoto.com; 38, AP Images/John Cogill; 39, Jim Richardson/NG Stock; 41, Stuart Monk/Alamy; 42, Paul van Riel/Hollandse Hoogte/Redux; 43, VALERIE KUYPERS/AFP/Getty Images; 44, Andy Rouse/naturepl.com; 45, O.DIGOIT/Alamy; 46, JTB MEDIA CREATION, Inc./Alamy; 47, CW Images/Alamy; 48, Bruno De Hogues/Getty Images; 49, PCN/Corbis; 51, *Bon Appetit*/Alamy; 52, Nigel Dickinson; 53, Luca da Ros/Grand Tour/Corbis; 54, Sandra Raccanello/SIME; 55, Massimo Ripani/SIME; 56, Craig Oesterling/NG My Shot; 57, Zoltan Nagy/SIME; 58-9, Owen Franken/Corbis; 60, Peter Turnley/Corbis; 61, imagebroker/Alamy; 62, Günter Gräfenhain/Huber/SIME; 63, Borderlands/Alamy; 64-5, Matt Moyer/NG Stock; 66, Bertrand Rieger/Hemis/Corbis; 67, Anders Ryman/Corbis; 69, Terry Eggers/Corbis; 70, Neil_Burton/iStockphoto; 71, Günter Gräfenhain/Huber/SIME; 72-3, KAMAL KISHORE/Reuters/Corbis; 74-5, kiyanochka/iStockphoto; 76, Orient/Huber/SIME; 77, JTB MEDIA CREATION, Inc./Alamy; 78-9, Richard Taylor/4Corners/SIME; 80,

Ugur OKUCU/Shutterstock; 81, Sasha Webb; 82, Mark Conlin/Getty Images; 83, Alaska Stock LLC/NG Stock; 84, Danita Delimont/Alamy; 85, Barrett Hedges/NG Stock; 87, WaterFrame/Alamy; 88, Steve Estvanik/Shutterstock.com; 89, Joel W. Rogers/Corbis; 90-91, Danita Delimont/Alamy; 92-3, Rich Reid/NG Stock; 94, David McNew/Getty Images; 95, AP Images/the *Record-Eagle,* Keith King; 97, BARBARA GINDL/epa/Corbis; 98, Marvin Dembinsky Photo Associates/Alamy; 99, Yves Marcoux/Getty Images; 100-101, Matt Currier Photography; 102, AJ Wilhelm/NG Stock; 103, Hemis/Alamy; 105, Buddy Mays/Alamy; 106-107, Medford Taylor/NG Stock; 108, Christian Heeb/laif/Redux; 109, Carolyn Brown/Photo Researchers/Getty Images; 110, Hemis/Alamy; 111, imagebroker/Alamy; 112-13, Keren Su/China Span/Alamy; 114, Ralph Lee Hopkins/NG Stock; 115, diddi@diddisig.is/Flickr/Getty Images; 117, Frans Lanting/NG Stock; 118, Marco Secchi/Alamy; 119, nagelestock.com/Alamy; 120, AdamEdwards/Shutterstock; 121, Jeff J Mitchell/Getty Images; 123, Gail Mooney/Corbis; 124, Pietro Canali/4Corners/SIME; 125, Albert Moldvay/NG Stock; 126-7, Ralph Lee Hopkins/NG Stock; 128, BOISVIEUX Christophe/hemis.fr/Getty Images; 129, Massimo Ripani/SIME; 130, Peter Essick/NG Stock; 131, Richard Manin/Hemis/Corbis; 132-3, Richard Belenos/Huber/SIME; 134, Richard Taylor/4Corners/SIME; 135, mediacolor's/Alamy; 136, Massimo Borchi/SIME; 137, Grant Rooney/Alamy; 139, Jens Schwarz/laif/Redux; 140-41, David Noton Photography/Alamy; 142, Sabine Lubenow/Getty Images; 143, Richard Du Toit/Minden Pictures/NG Stock; 144-5, Chris Bolin/First Light/Getty Images; 146, Guenter Guni/iStockphoto; 147, Frans Lanting/NG Stock; 148, Monica Gumm/laif/Redux Pictures; 149, Justin Foulkes/4Corners/SIME; 150, Van Berge, Alexander/the food passionates/Corbis; 151, Michael Melford/NG Stock; 152, Bruno Morandi/Getty Images; 153, Walter Bibikow/Getty Images; 154, amana images inc./Alamy; 155, Rothenborg Kyle/Getty Images; 156-7, Fred Bavendam/Minden Pictures/NG Stock; 158, Peter Walton Photography/Getty Images; 159, Photograph by David Messent/Getty Images; 160, David Wall/Alamy; 161,

Doug Pearson/JAI/Corbis; 162-3, Giovanni Simeone/SIME; 164, Inga Spence/Alamy; 165, Jodi Cobb/NG Stock; 166-7, P Robin Moeller/iStockphoto.com; 168, Blaine Harrington III/Corbis; 169, Rolf Nussbaumer Photography/Alamy; 170-1, Paul Nicklen/NG Stock; 172, Allen Fredrickson/Icon SMI/Corbis; 173, Kevin R. Morris/Corbis; 174-5, H. Mark Weidman Photography/Alamy; 176, Doug Wilson/Alamy; 177, Pete Ryan/NG Stock; 179, Martin Thomas Photography/Alamy; 180, Chris Murray/Aurora/Getty Images; 181, Tyler Nordgren; 182-3, Michael Melford/NG Stock; 184-5, Bill O'Leary/the *Washington Post* via Getty Images; 186, Corbis; 187, Reinhard Dirscherl/Alamy; 188, AP Images/Marco Ugarte; 189, Dordo Brnobic/NG My Shot; 190, Sebastian Giacobone/Shutterstock; 191, Michael & Jennifer Lewis/NG Stock; 192, Dave Donaldson/Alamy; 193, Benoit Jacquelin/iStockphoto; 195, Cephas Picture Library/Alamy; 196, John Miller/Robert Harding World Imagery/Corbis; 197, Heiko Specht/laif/Redux; 198, Intrepix/Shutterstock.com; 199, CAMERA PRESS/Sergey Pyatakov/RIA Novosti/Redux; 200, Greg Dale/NG Stock; 201, Reinhard Schmid/Huber/SIME; 203, oktoberfestbrisbane.com.au; 204, imagebroker.net/SuperStock; 205, ARCO/C Bömke/age fotostock; 206, KIKETXO/Shutterstock; 207, Guido Cozzi/SIME; 208, Reinhard Schmid/Huber/SIME; 209, Yonatan Sindel/Flash90/Redux; 210-211, Dave Yoder; 212, NHPA/SuperStock; 213, Danita Delimont/Gallo Images/Getty Images; 215, Francois Lacasse/NHLI via Getty Images; 216, Huw Jones/4Corners/SIME; 217, Danita Delimont/Getty Images; 218, Alfred Cheng Jin/Reuters/Corbis; 219, imagebroker/Alamy; 220, Michael Yamashita/NG Stock; 221, PONGMANAT TASIRI/epa/Corbis; 223, Travelasia/Asia Images/Corbis; 224-5, Joseph J. Hobbs; 226, Dave Stamboulis/Alamy; 227, Michael Leach/Getty Images; 228-9, Roy Samuelsen/NG My Shot; 230, Alaska Photography/Flickr/Getty Images; 231, Rolf Hicker/All Canada Photos/Getty Images; 233, Joe McBride/Getty Images; 234, Chao Kusollerschariya/NG My Shot; 235, Diane Cook & Len Jenshel/Corbis; 236, Bill Hatcher/NG Stock; 237, Michael Rubin/iStockphoto; 238-9, Jeffrey Noble/Photo of Derrick

Suwaima Davis (Hopi/Choctaw), six-time World Hoop Dance Champion/Courtesy of Scottsdale Convention & Visitors Bureau; 240, Nik Wheeler/Corbis; 241, Evan Richman/the *Boston Globe* via Getty Images; 242, Patrick Batchelder/Alamy; 243, Irek/4Corners/SIME; 244, Michael S. Yamashita/NG Stock; 245, Cora/Bildagentur Schapowalow/SIME; 247, STR/AFP/Getty Images; 248, Used with permission from The Biltmore Company, Asheville, North Carolina; 249, Doug Perrine/Getty Images; 250-51, Shane Pinder/Alamy; 252-3, Günter Gräfenhain/Huber/SIME; 254, Orlando Barria/epa/Corbis; 255, Kenneth Garrett/NG Stock; 256-7, Medford Taylor/NG Stock; 258, Konrad Wothe/Minden Pictures/NG Stock; 259, Mike Theiss/NG Stock; 260, Raymond Choo/NG My Shot; 261, John Stanmeyer LLC/NG Stock; 262, Giordano Cipriani/SIME; 263, Catarina Belova/Shutterstock.com; 265, Bernd Römmelt/Huber/SIME; 266, Travelscape Images/Alamy; 267, O. Louis Mazzatenta/NG Stock; 268, Michael S. Lewis/NG Stock; 269, Yadid Levy/Photolibrary/Getty Images; 270, Yadid Levy/Anzenberger/Redux Pictures; 271, Eduardo Longoni/Corbis; 272-3, Horizons WWP/Alamy; 274-5, Frank Lukasseck/Corbis; 276, DEA/G. DAGLI ORT/Getty Images; 277, Press Association via AP Images; 278, Colin Dutton/SIME; 279, John Lamb/Getty Images; 280-81, Massimo Ripani/Grand Tour/Corbis; 282, Massimo Borchi/SIME; 283, Gregor Lengler/laif/Redux; 285, Anna Watson/Corbis; 286, Rune Rormyr/NG My Shot; 287, Stefan Volk/laif/Redux; 288, Emportes Jm/Getty Images; 289, Berthold Steinhilber/laif/Redux; 290-91, Guido Cozzi/SIME; 292, Martin Siepmann/imagebroker/Corbis; 293, Kajano/Shutterstock; 295, Lew Robertson/Getty Images; 296, Mandy Glinsbockel/Demotix/Corbis; 297, Guido Cozzi/SIME; 298, Allen Woodman/NG My Shot; 299, Eric Isselee/Shutterstock; 300, Imaginechina/Corbis; 301, Otto Stadler/Huber/SIME; 302, LOOK Die Bildagentur der Fotografen GmbH/Alamy; 303, Blaine Harrington III/Corbis; 305, HP Huber/Huber/SIME; 306-307, John Eastcott and Yva Momatiuk/NG Stock; 306, DJ Spooky; 308, Paul Abbitt rf/Alamy; 309, Tui De Roy/Minden Pictures/NG Stock.

Four Seasons of Travel

400 OF THE WORLD'S BEST DESTINATIONS IN WINTER, SPRING, SUMMER, AND FALL

Published by the National Geographic Society

John M. Fahey, *Chairman of the Board and Chief Executive Officer*

Declan Moore, *Executive Vice President; President, Publishing and Travel*

Melina Gerosa Bellows, *Executive Vice President; Chief Creative Officer, Books, Kids, and Family*

Lynn Cutter, *Executive Vice President, Travel*

Keith Bellows, *Senior Vice President and Editor in Chief, National Geographic Travel Media*

Prepared by the Book Division

Hector Sierra, *Senior Vice President and General Manager*

Janet Goldstein, *Senior Vice President and Editorial Director*

Jonathan Halling, *Design Director, Books and Children's Publishing*

Marianne R. Koszorus, *Design Director, Books*

Barbara A. Noe, *Senior Editor, National Geographic Travel Books*

R. Gary Colbert, *Production Director*

Jennifer A. Thornton, *Director of Managing Editorial*

Susan S. Blair, *Director of Photography*

Meredith C. Wilcox, *Director, Administration and Rights Clearance*

Staff for This Book

Lawrence M. Porges, *Editor*

Carol Clurman, *Project Editor*

Elisa Gibson, *Art Director*

Nancy Marion, *Illustrations Editor*

Jennifer Pocock, Rhett Register, *Researchers*

Carl Mehler, *Director of Maps*

XNR Productions, *Map Research and Production*

Mark Baker, Larry Bleiberg, Karen Carmichael, Maryellen Duckett, Olivia Garnett, Adam Graham, Jeremy Gray, Graeme Green, Rachael Jackson, Tim Jepson, Justin Kavanagh, Margaret Loftus, Michael Luongo, Jenna Makowski, Barbara A. Noe, Christine O'Toole, Gabrielle Piccininni, Ed Readicker-Henderson, Emma Rowley, Jenna Schnuer, Kelsey Snell, Olivia Stren, Phil Trupp, Joe Yogerst, *Contributing Writers*

Marshall Kiker, *Associate Managing Editor*

Judith Klein, *Production Editor*

Mike Horenstein, *Production Manager*

Galen Young, *Rights Clearance Specialist*

Katie Olsen, *Production Design Assistant*

Sarah Alban, Danielle Fisher, Jane Plegge, Marlena Serviss, *Contributors*

Production Services

Phillip L. Schlosser, *Senior Vice President*

Chris Brown, *Vice President, NG Book Manufacturing*

George Bounelis, *Vice President, Production Services*

Nicole Elliott, *Manager*

Rachel Faulise, *Manager*

Robert L. Barr, *Manager*

Learning Resource Centre
Stockton Riverside College

CELEBRATING ‹125› YEARS

The National Geographic Society is one of the world's largest nonprofit scientific and educational organizations. Founded in 1888 to "increase and diffuse geographic knowledge," the Society works to inspire people to care about the planet. National Geographic reflects the world through its magazines, television programs, films, music and radio, books, DVDs, maps, exhibitions, live events, school publishing programs, interactive media and merchandise. *National Geographic* magazine, the Society's official journal, published in English and 33 local-language editions, is read by more than 60 million people each month. The National Geographic Channel reaches 435 million households in 37 languages in 173 countries. National Geographic Digital Media receives more than 19 million visitors a month. National Geographic has funded more than 10,000 scientific research, conservation and exploration projects and supports an education program promoting geography literacy. For more information, visit www.nationalgeographic.com.

For more information, please call 1-800-NGS LINE (647-5463) or write to the following address:

National Geographic Society
1145 17th Street N.W.
Washington, D.C. 20036-4688 U.S.A.

For information about special discounts for bulk purchases, please contact National Geographic Books Special Sales: ngspecsales@ngs.org

For rights or permissions inquiries, please contact National Geographic Books Subsidiary Rights: ngbookrights@ngs.org

Copyright © 2013 National Geographic Society
All rights reserved. Reproduction of the whole or any part of the contents without written permission from the publisher is prohibited.

Library of Congress Cataloging-in-Publication Data
National Geographic Society (U.S.)
  Four seasons of travel : 400 of the world's best destinations in winter, spring, summer, and fall / National Geographic Books ; foreword by Andrew Evans, National Geographic Traveler magazine contributing editor and "Digital Nomad".
    pages cm
  Includes index.
  ISBN 978-1-4262-1167-6 (hardcover : alk. paper)
  1. Voyages and travels. I. Title.
  G465.N365 2013
  910.4--dc23
                              2013010861

Printed in China

13/CCOS/1

The information in this book has been carefully checked and to the best of our knowledge is accurate. However, details are subject to change, and the National Geographic Society cannot be responsible for such changes, or for errors or omissions.